COTTAGE GARDENING
IN TOWN & COUNTRY

COTTAGE GARDENING
IN TOWN & COUNTRY

Philip Swindells

Salem House Publishers
Topsfield, Massachusetts

First published in the United States by Salem House
Publishers, 1986
462 Boston Street, Topsfield, MA 01983

Library of Congress Catalog Card Number: 86-60717

ISBN: 0 88162 206 0

Printed and bound in Italy by G. Canale and Co SpA

CONTENTS

PREFACE

Unruly plants growing in tangled informality. Sweet fragrances, soft colours, the hum of bees and the flutter of butterflies. Perhaps the gentle whisper of leaves or the murmur of water. Add these to a neat white cottage with a thatched roof where apple blossom never fades and the sun always shines and we have a cottage garden. Take away the perpetual apple blossom and constant sunshine, substitute the cottage for your own home and I present to you the subject of this book.

Traditional cottage gardens do not need a traditional cottage for them to be a reality. Any plot, no matter what shape, size or soil type can be transformed into a garden of the traditional English cottage type. Transformation is not a problem, but maintenance may be, for cottage gardens are the most labour intensive imaginable if a chocolate box image is desired. So before you undertake such an enterprise it is imperative that you allow sufficient time to maintain what you create. A badly tended cottage garden is a disaster, a properly cared for one a delight.

P.S.

ACKNOWLEDGEMENTS

All the colour photographs were taken by Bob Challinor.

The publishers are grateful to The National Gardens Scheme and to the following Hon. County Organizers of the Scheme for suggesting suitable gardens to illustrate the book: Lady Heald (Surrey), Mrs R. Clay (Gwent), J. Morris Esq. (North-East Hampshire), Mrs D. Hodges (Oxfordshire), Mrs A. Hardy (Kent), Mrs B. Jones (Greater London) and Mrs A. Sanford (Gloucestershire). The publishers are also particularly grateful to the following garden owners for granting permission for their gardens to be photographed: Mr & Mrs G. Bunting (pp. 21, 59 & 61), Mr & Mrs J. Chambers (pp. 39 (lower) & 75), Mrs R. Clay (pp. 39 (top) & 93), Rev. & Mrs R. B. Feast (frontispiece, pp. 15, 45 & 77), Mrs Z. Grant (pp. 19, 35 & 49), Miss H. O'Kelly & Miss B. Harper (p. 53), Mr & Mrs P. Hickman (p. 43), Mr & Mrs W. May (pp. 55 (lower), 65, 97 (lower) & 105), Mr & Mrs J. Morris (p. 89), Mr & Mrs A. E. Pedder (pp. 55 (top) & 102), Mrs S. Rainforth (pp. 31 & 33), Mr & Mrs R. Raworth (pp. 51, 69 (lower) & 97 (upper)), Mrs B. Shuker & Miss Strange (pp. 69 (upper) & 83), Mr & Mrs D. Simmons (pp. 23, 71, 73 & 95), Mrs A. M. Sitwell (pp. 40 & 75), Mr & Mrs A. N. Sturt (pp. 85 & 101) and Mr & Mrs J. Whistler (p. 27).

The line drawings were drawn by Nils Solberg.

Fig. 5 is after the illustrations on p. 146, *The Low Maintenance Garden*, G. Rose, Windward; Fig. 7 is after the illustrations on p. 11, *Making the Most of Clematis*, R. Evison, Floraprint, 1979; and Fig. 10 is after the illustration on p. 18, *Bulbs*, C. Grey-Wilson & B. Mathew, Collins, 1981.

1
MAKING A START

There is no such thing as a standard cottage garden. Every person's idea of what one should be has been tempered or enhanced by the experiences of life. Some may have been fortunate enough to have grown up in a cottage with a traditional garden, or maybe in a village where cottage gardens were a part of everyday life. For others a cottage garden may have always been a dream – fanciful visions created by chocolate boxes and jigsaw puzzles.

No matter how you became interested in the concept of a cottage garden, or how practical or fanciful your ideas may be, they will all embrace certain unshakeable criteria – that the garden should be homely, informal, colourful and fragrant. How these criteria are fulfilled will vary widely and it is not my purpose to impose ideas upon the reader. I see my role here as providing a practical introduction to the concept. Presenting the reader with a canvas – the raw outlines and materials of his garden – then offering him the paints – flowers, shrubs and trees – so that he can create his very own picture. How he arranges this is his own personal pleasure.

It can be said from the beginning though, that no attempt to create such a garden should be made without an overall plan of campaign in mind. It is a wise gardener who makes a plan to cover a set period of time and then adheres to it as closely as possible.

REVIEWING THE SITE

The first task to be undertaken is the study of any existing trees, hedges and buildings that are likely to affect the growing of specific plants or the creation of special features.

Tall hedges and overhanging trees wherever possible should receive suitable pruning in order to allow access for sunlight and the free passage of air. Buildings are a permanent feature, but ways in which they can be used if forming the boundary, or any benefits that can be derived through sheltering plants from the wind, shading those that desire it, or by reflecting heat from their walls should be thoroughly investigated.

Few plants really appreciate shade and where this is unavoidable the siting of a garden shed or compost heap can use ground unsuitable for planting. This must of course tie in with an overall plan, but the positioning of sheds and compost heaps in the shade while ensuring an open sunny position for glasshouse and frame is essential. Paths servicing these buildings should be decided afterwards, not as is often the case before construction, as then the buildings are placed where the paths have been laid.

Soil 'profile'/soil levels

Before a definite plan can be drawn up it is advisable to take a soil 'profile'. This is broadly speaking a hole which is dug sufficiently deep to expose to view the varying layers of material that form the top 60–90 cm (2–3 ft) of soil and thus has a bearing upon operations such as drainage which may be necessary before serious gardening can begin.

The approximate relationships of different levels to one another and the house are also important. By taking a good stout plank of wood devoid of twists and unevenness, a handful of strong wooden stakes and a spirit level, a reasonably accurate picture can be obtained. The board is used on edge with the spirit level lying along the upper edge. Stakes are then progressively knocked into the ground at slightly less distance than the board's length. A definite fixed level such as the back door step is taken as a starting point and a stake knocked into the ground so that the board and spirit level can be rested on both step and stake, the latter being knocked slowly into the ground until the board and spirit level show a level reading (Fig. 1). The end of the board that rested on the step is placed on the stake and another stake pushed into the ground at a suitable distance and in the same manner. From each of these stakes fresh ones can be put in level so

plants in their shadow or the free flow of air around them. Great care is necessary in altering such barriers when they form a common boundary with a neighbour, and his co-operation should be sought from the outset. On a new garden where no such barriers exist, except perhaps for the concrete posts and strands of wire erected by the builder, advantage can be taken of the fact and suitable materials used to form a boundary of overall benefit to the garden.

Fencing panels of the well-known overlapping kind can be used to great effect in sheltering the garden from cold northern and eastern winds, and yet at the same time

Fig 1. Soil levels. Taking a fixed level such as a doorstep, the lie of the land can be ascertained by using pegs, straight edge and a spirit level.

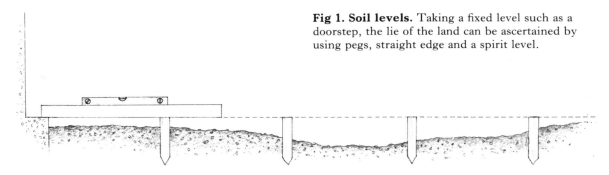

that the overall effect is diamond or triangular patterns of level stakes, which if connected by strings attached to small tacks on their tops will reveal the true lie of the land beneath.

Of course this method is not one hundred per cent accurate and to do the job properly back checking with the board from certain 'master' stakes to the others will ensure that the minimum of error is transmitted from one to the other. However, it is a good general guide as to how the ground rises and falls, facts extremely difficult to ascertain with the naked eye.

Boundaries

The boundary of the property is another important factor to consider when surveying the site. Established gardens have hedges and fences of varying types which it is undesirable to tamper with unless they restrict light to such an extent that it affects

provide support for climbing plants. A southerly or westerly aspect would automatically be available when sheltering the garden from the north and east and these may be additionally used to accommodate slightly tender plants. Natural barriers such as hedges and screens of quickthorn or privet have much to commend them. All allow for the free passage of air and those of a thorny nature are virtually animal-proof as well. Additionally they are pleasing to the eye, but it must be said that they require attention in the way of clipping and also deplete the soil of plant foods within a considerable distance of their base. However, I am a strong advocate of a good hedge in the cottage garden. Not only does it provide an excellent foil for gaudy border plants, but can throw up some surprises as we shall see.

Simple wooden fences of an open character have their uses, allowing air and light to pass through freely, and with a cottage garden give joy to the passer-by, exposing the garden picture to view. Brick walls have the opposite effect in giving a greater measure of privacy, but they cannot be recommended. The soil at the base of a wall is invariably dry, dusty and almost inert unless given very careful attention. The concrete footing often interferes with cultivations and apart from the obvious virtue of little maintenance there is not much that can be said in favour of walling.

GETTING IDEAS ON PAPER

It is advisable before picking up a spade to make an outline plan on paper. This not only records one's thoughts, but puts the garden more into perspective than when one paces out areas for pergolas or borders with irregular strides. The shape of the garden once drawn on paper is often not as you think, and the various levels of the soil in different parts of the garden can be quite a revelation.

Outline plan

Graph paper is a useful material to use on which to draw the plan, for then each square can represent a fixed measurement and the ordinary mortal can make a more accurate drawing than is the case if he is encumbered with protractors, set squares and a plain sheet of paper. Existing features should be marked, and for a realistic appraisal of the situation, a few scale cut-outs in card of large trees, buildings or any other features of the immediate landscape should be made and erected on the plan. This gives an idea of the effect each feature will have on the garden and the best way to overcome or utilize it. The placing of any buildings should be decided and the position of paths drawn in.

Paths should not be skimped, for although they occupy valuable ground, they are the lifeline of the garden and should be

adequate and in good repair. One good wide path sufficient to take a wheelbarrow with ease is preferable to half a dozen narrow ones where the handles will catch in the plants on either side. A bold sweeping gravel path with elegant curves can be the making of a cottage garden. Not only visually, but as a main artery to its heart, thus ensuring relative ease of maintenance irrespective of weather conditions.

The placing of trees and bushes should also be carefully considered, for once successfully established they resent disturbance. Ample distance should be allowed for them to mature successfully and recommended distances adhered to. Half standard trees may look better planted a couple of metres (yards) apart when received from the nursery, but within four or five years will intermingle and become a terrible mess incapable of proper care and cultivation unless thinned to the recommended distance. Close planting of woody plants to paths should similarly be avoided, at least the recommended distance between plants being applied in the same manner between plants and path.

The proximity of plants to the house also deserves consideration. Utility subjects like thyme and mint that are both decorative and frequently used in the kitchen should be placed as close to the door as feasible. Every square metre of soil capable of supporting plant life should be utilized, for this is the concept of a cottage garden. An odd bit by the garden shed may support a rambling rose, the narrow border alongside the house or garage perhaps a fan-trained cherry. In fact the opportunities for inventiveness in planting are legion.

Having decided upon the position which each permanent feature will take and having marked it carefully on the plan, the next important aspect to consider is the various levels of the plot and the method of drainage to be employed if this should prove necessary. Steeply sloping ground may be difficult to work and heavy rain may lead to erosion of the top soil. This can be remedied by terracing, using one or maybe two retaining walls and then levelling the soil into two or three plateaux. Uneven ground, if marked out with stakes of even height, is relatively simple to level into gentle slopes and rises which are easy on the eye, the back, and the barrow. However, it is imperative on the plan to be clear as to which way the land falls, or more important, is likely to fall after necessary correction, before a drainage scheme is devised.

Planning the drainage

Normally this need not be a complicated affair, for the average garden is not vast, and no more than two or possibly three tracks will be required to ensure adequate drainage. It is illegal to connect land drainage to the public sewer or even the thick gravel bed which these drains rest on. In most cases it would be impractical to do so even if this were possible, and so it is wise to consult one's own deeds or local documents to try and discover where common drains run. Perhaps there is a brook close by, or maybe a parish ditch into which surface water may flow. When a discovery of this type is successfully made, then the disposal of water seldom present any problems. However, if you are less fortunate, the use of one or possibly two soakaways (large pits filled with rubble, then topped with firm soil), if not entirely over-coming the drainage problem, will do much to alleviate water-logging. Before anything is started though, take a look at your soil type – the raw ingredient of the garden.

A LOOK AT THE SOIL

There are two common types of soil; light and heavy. Light soil is light in weight, not light in colour and of a rather coarse texture with large particles – of sand chiefly – containing large air spaces which prevent them from packing tightly. Large air spaces assist with the free passage of water which in times of drought gives rise to very rapid

drying. Heavy soils are composed of very fine particles which pack closely together. They hold moisture readily, and very quickly become caked and sticky, or when dried out set into a cement-like lump.

To improve light soils, moisture-holding materials such as cow or pig manure, or old leaves and compost, should be incorporated. Artificial fertilizer should only be used during the active growing season, for if applied during winter the rain will almost certainly wash it out of the soil before it has an opportunity to work. Regular hoeing during the summer assists with retaining moisture, while surface mulches of old leaves or rotted lawn mowings around individual plants are most beneficial.

Heavy soils, conversely, require lightening and opening up. This can be done by digging in quantities of straw, strawy manure, sand, grit, clinker or indeed any other material of a coarse texture. On clay soils with a relatively low alkalinity, hydrated lime can be used. When spread evenly over the soil surface and then lightly raked in it causes flocculation of the clay particles – the collecting and separating of colonies of tiny particles which under the physical influence of the lime form larger particles, which in turn makes the soil lighter.

Soils of many varying textures and constituents exist, such as peaty, alluvial, marl, and others too numerous to consider, but all can be classified with some degree of accuracy under the heading of light or heavy. However, apart from visible physical characteristics there are those unseen, particularly acidity and alkalinity, which are of equal importance but more difficult to ascertain. A pH test – obtainable in kit form from the local garden shop – has to be employed to determine the acidity or alkalinity of the soil. The theory and reasoning behind this is complex and irrelevant at this stage, but it is sufficient to say that a pH of 7.0 indicates a neutral soil, one higher, say of 8.0 alkaline, and those of lower numerals acid. Careful observation of local wild flowers will also yield much information.

Where heather, foxgloves and sorrel flourish the soil is invariably acid, but where vetches, cranesbills and old man's beard thrive then it will almost certainly be alkaline. These conditions can have a marked effect upon plant growth; where such conditions may pertain, I will discuss them.

PREPARING THE SITE

Having surveyed the site as suggested earlier and made a provisional plan, or even a few sketchy notes on paper, it is time to don gumboots and gardening gloves and get outside. The best way to tackle the job is to cut down any offending overhanging branches, thick or floppy hedges and long undergrowth and then prepare a bonfire. In a new or neglected garden this clearance will generally reveal all manner of miscellanea. Solid materials that may prove useful as the foundations of paths should be heaped neatly in a corner. Such items are bricks, broken tiles, lumps of concrete and large stones. Burnable rubbish should be consigned to the bonfire and metal objects and other similar items such as old bottles be placed in the dustbin or taken to the local tip.

Constructing the drainage

The levels of the site must now be considered and the drainage scheme laid. The manner in which surface levels can be discovered was described earlier, and any undesirable lumps and hollows should be levelled out with a spade. Drainage can then be undertaken, the method and materials employed being more directly related to the wealth of the individual than the type of soil or fall of land involved.

Tile drains laid in a herring-bone fashion are undoubtedly the most satisfactory and permanent of all methods, but it goes without saying that they are by far the most expensive, and can only be regarded as the sole suitable means of drainage on lighter soils. Tile drains are small lengths of clay

pipes, commonly used by the agricultural community, which are laid in trenches on top of a generous layer of stones or pea-shingle (Fig. 2). Laid properly they form a quick and efficient means of drainage, only causing trouble if laid unevenly when silting will occur, or when used near vigorous trees such as poplar or willow whose roots have an uncanny knack of locating the pipes and travelling inside them until eventually they

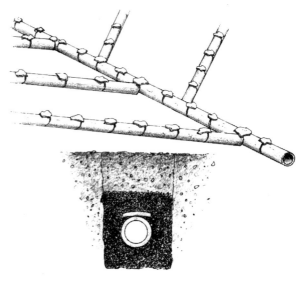

Fig 2. Drainage. (*a*) Tile drains in a herring-bone pattern. Lateral drains should join the main track slightly askance from one another. Broken pieces of pipe cover the joints to prevent silting up. (*b*) For the best effect tile drains are laid on a bed of pea-shingle.

occupy the entire bore. Other methods are suitable on medium to heavy land, for then the soil assists by being sufficiently stiff to support itself.

The layout of the drains, of no matter what kind, should follow a set pattern to ensure even withdrawal of excess water from the soil. One or two main trenches can run the length of the garden, or a single track diagonally across the garden from upper to lower opposite corners. These tracks should fall towards the outlet point and be of larger bore than their subsidiaries. These branch pipes join the main track in a herring-bone fashion being at approximately forty-five degrees to the main track and joining slightly askance from one another. If they join directly opposite one another silting occurs and the drains eventually become blocked.

Permanent features

The site having been cleared and subterranean activities ceased, careful consideration should be given to permanent features such as the shed, greenhouse and paths, for once a decision is made regarding their siting little can be done to alter the original intention without a major upheaval. Although you may not consider erecting either a shed or greenhouse immediately, the space allocated to them should be marked out and kept free of weeds until such time as this is possible. Paths, however, are a different matter, for it is virtually impossible to run a well ordered garden without at least one clean level path.

The boundaries, which will have been considered when surveying the site, should be put in good order or repaired before any substantial works commence, and any trees that are required ordered from the nurseryman for delivery at the appropriate time. My point here regarding ordering and planting long term subjects early on in the development, is that they can be growing while other work is going on. It is advisable therefore to plan the siting of trees, especially in a new garden very early in the proceedings so that they can be established as quickly as possible.

Digging

These essential preliminaries having been completed, the basis of a successful garden will lie before one. Irrespective of the time of year that the garden is started, it is a good policy to turn up uncultivated soil in hefty lumps to allow it to weather. Most advantage will be gained by autumn digging, for then weeds will have little chance to grow and the frost and rain can work on the soil eroding and fragmenting it so that when spring comes it will knock down into a powdery tilth. Done properly, with all the top growth buried, digging will dispose of at least half the weeds on the surface of the plot.

Perennial weeds with deep roots such as thistles, dock and bindweed should be pulled out where practicable and subsequently burned. Where infestation is bad, the worst should be removed and the emerging shoots killed in the spring with a suitable weedkiller, or else the plants grown on that area spaced far enough apart to allow regular hoeing to remove the weeds as they appear. Few weeds survive for long if their shoots are regularly decapitated.

On the other hand though, the use of a rotavator amongst weeds of this type can lead unwittingly to proliferation, the rotors chopping the roots into tiny pieces which will then shoot and grow into separate entities. No method of initial weed control is perfect, but much can be achieved by sensible digging.

Most textbooks on gardening reveal a lot of nonsense and non-practice by their exponents on the digging operation. Double digging, single digging, bastard trenching and several other kinds are all described, together with complicated diagrams showing plot A and plot B and how the soil from the trench on plot A should be wheeled to the far end of plot B for replacement at the end of digging operations. Gardeners are generally practical people, and while erring on the side of caution when anything new is revealed, usually pick out the best bits of both old and new methods and come to a compromise. It is my opinion that few gardeners do not realize the folly of double digging (i.e. the digging and breaking up of soil two spades deep), but most do appreciate the value that single digging and trenching can have if applied sensibly.

Single digging is merely the turning over or completely inverting a lump of soil so that the surface covered with plant growth is at the bottom of the spit. This is only performed on well-cultivated ground, being unsuitable for use when rough land is involved. This needs trenching in order to knock it into shape, the first row being inverted as with single digging, and the second row inverted on top of the first (Fig. 3). An open trench is now revealed which will accept each row of digging as the soil is turned over. Turned over is the operative word, for weeds will not die if the spadeful is merely tipped on one side, reversal must be complete. My slightly unconventional method of starting trenching leads to a raised first row and a trench at the end of the bed, but this is of no account as the trench facilitates drainage during the winter and is easily filled when the soil is knocked down and raked level. This latter inconvenience is nothing compared with the interminable barrowing of soil which the purists would have us do.

A bare border or bed waiting to be dug is a formidable and disheartening spectacle even for the most ardent gardener, and breaking with convention once more, I have found that a little personal psychology can ease the somewhat distressing state of mind that a newcomer in particular may suffer. First of all do not tackle the job all at once, take it in stages building each day's digging upon the next so that the neat brown rows seem to grow, or as one old gardener told me: 'When digging always keep your back to the ground you have yet to dig!' This latter remark although seemingly frivolous, has a moral, and that is not to look at the bed in its entirety, but concentrate on the piece you can manage that day. I find it a big help to kid yourself that you are actually digging faster than you are by taking narrow strips a metre (yard) or so wide and digging the full length of the bed. Obviously the ground is not covered any faster, but the illusion is that this is so.

Fig 3. Trenching.

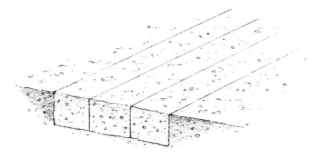

(a) Sequence of rows to be dug.

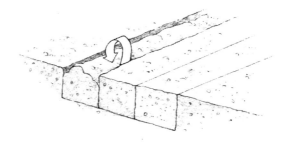

(b) The first row is inverted upon itself.

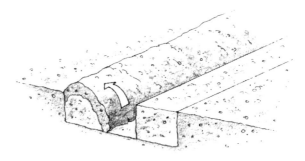

(c) The second row is inverted upon the first.

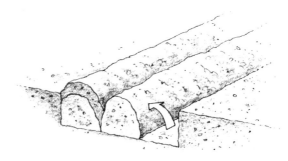

(d) The third row is inverted in the trench created by the removal of the second row. This is repeated until the plot is dug.

13

2

SHRUBS AND ROSES

We can now look at the diversity of plant material that is available to the cottage gardener. And where better to start than among the shrubs and roses. Let us not get carried away on a tide of nostalgia though, before we consider one of the most important features in the garden – the hedge. A living barrier, often despised for the work that it creates, but a utility feature of practical benefit and visual pleasure.

A LOOK AT HEDGES

When considering hedges within a cottage garden we are not necessarily thinking about hedges as external boundaries, although we must give them careful thought. We should not close our eyes to the use of non-functional barriers of attractive low growing subjects which can perhaps be used to edge a path or bed.

A selection of hedging plants

Lavender comes immediately to mind when discussing such propositions, particularly neat compact cultivars like 'Munstead Dwarf' and 'Baby White'. The former is a smaller version of the traditional old English lavender, but rarely grows more than 45 cm (1½ ft) high, while 'Baby White' is of similar stature with blossoms of icy-white. *Lavandula* 'Loddon Pink' provides a further colour variation, and *L. stoechas* an earlier flowering period. This will be in flower during early summer, at least a couple of months ahead of its cousins. All respond well to clipping, a necessity during late summer if they are to be kept in order.

The same applies for rosemary, *Rosmarinus officinalis*, and although not

perhaps considered to be a suitable candidate for hedging, in its upright form, known as 'Miss Jessup', it is superb. Try mixing rosemary with lavender in a ratio of one rosemary to three or four lavender and you will have a lovely dwarf informal hedge. If you think that this sounds bizarre, see the excellent example at the Cambridge University Botanic Garden.

Cotton lavenders can be used too, particularly *Santolina chamaecyparissus* with its soft grey aromatic foliage and curious disc-like flowers. *Santolina neapolitana* is also most attractive, but to my mind is not tight enough for a really neat hedge, while *S. viridis* can do the job, but being bright green is not to everyone's taste.

Prunus cistena 'Crimson Dwarf' on the other hand is really quite startling. With deep purple foliage and dazzling white flowers, this is a taller hedge and can be used equally well internally or as a boundary, although it loses its leaves for the winter. It can be maintained as a barrier at around one metre (one yard), the same height as can be achieved by the dwarf Russian almond, *P. tenella*, a little gem with bright pink flowers and fresh green leaves. While coloured foliage forms of *P. cerasifera* like 'Trailblazer' and 'Vesuvius' can be recommended for more substantial barriers.

The opportunities for exploiting various shrubby plants for hedging are tremendous. We do not need to stick to common privet, *Ligustrum ovalifolium* and that dreadful, dusty and boring evergreen *Lonicera nitida*. This makes a quick barrier it is true and can be planted in a golden leafed form as well, but it grows like fury and requires constant attention. Then once well established, it opens up completely with the first

Conifers provide a backbone for this garden while splashes of colour are
provided by the plants carpeting the ground.

substantial snowfall. When choosing a boundary hedge be a little more ambitious. Providing that you do not go over the top completely the cottage garden illusion will remain intact.

If you garden in a cold area then try *Berberis darwinii*. With its small glossy, evergreen, holly-like foliage it makes an impenetrable barrier that is secure against animals and small boys alike. When neatly clipped the attractive orange coloured blossoms are not so freely produced, but there are enough to create interest and these are followed by bunches of tiny grape-like fruits. Common holly, *Ilex aquifolium*, can be used in the same manner and displays similar characteristics to *Berberis darwinii* when grown as a hedge. For something really interesting and historically in context, try using the slower growing and more spiny hedgehog holly, *Ilex aquifolium* 'Ferox'. This is a handsome shrub of dense growth with small twisted and puckered leaves that are armed with short sharp spines around the edges and on the face of the blade.

Many deciduous flowering shrubs that we usually grow free-standing in the garden make interesting and attractive hedging subjects, for example the common *Forsythia intermedia* 'Spectabilis'. When in full flower during the spring it is a joy to behold, a vivid band of rich golden yellow that gradually pales to soft green as its leaves unfurl. Unfortunately this effect is lost during the winter, but the dense growth created by a well grown and clipped forsythia hedge makes this little more than an irritation.

The same applies to the lilac honeysuckle, *Lonicera syringantha*, for this too is deciduous, but capable of dense twiggy growth if properly maintained. I can never understand why this most desirable hedging plant with its pleasant bluish-green leaves and fragrant soft lilac flowers is not more widely planted.

Many of the cotoneasters can be adapted to hedge culture, but there are two that are particularly suitable. The first is the ubiquitous *Cotoneaster simonsii*, an upright vase-shaped semi-evergreen with bright scarlet or orange berries. When grown as a hedge it forms a dense barrier which can be clipped in the same way as privet, but with the added bonus of autumn berries which seem to appear even when the plants are harshly clipped. However, my favourite is *C. lacteus*, an informal hedging plant with graceful arching branches of downy green foliage which support masses of creamy-white blossoms. These are followed in the autumn by bright red berries which persist for much of the winter. Its uses are to some degree restricted by its habit, but where informality is the keynote it should be given due consideration.

Escallonias are not widely accepted as hedging plants, yet they grow reasonably quickly and flower when quite closely clipped. Sadly they have the reputation of being maritime plants and not so suited to inland conditions. This is untrue of course and very sad, for although escallonias cannot always be relied upon to be completely and reliably evergreen in colder parts of the country, they always do well, especially *Escallonia macrantha*. A big bold evergreen with strangely aromatic foliage and deep carmine blossoms, this is one of the tougher kinds and for most winters is reliably evergreen with me. The cultivar 'Crimson Spire' is equally resilient, but is hard pressed to yield a hedge of any substance once more than a metre (yard) high.

This is a problem too with the New Zealand daisy bush, *Olearia haastii*. For the most part olearias are regarded as tender. While this is the case with a few species it does not apply to *O. haastii* or its parents *O. avicennifolia* and *O. moschata*, both flourishing with me in a hostile Yorkshire garden.

When a closely cropped hedge is necessary, and despite the general theme of informality in the cottage garden there are cases for its introduction, then use common box, *Buxus sempervirens*. This is a well known evergreen with tiny rounded glossy leaves that was formerly used for low hedging. It will produce a sizeable hedge, albeit slowly, but if properly maintained will last for years. Some gardeners feel that it is rather drab and dusty. If you are one of these then how about experimenting with one or two of its cultivars. For example, the creamy-white variegated *B. sempervirens* 'Argentea' and the irregularly margined 'Elegantissima'.

The most important thing to discover would be the response of these fancy cultivars to close clipping. Would this lead to the foliage reverting to its original green form, or rather the dominance of green over variegated? Gardening is full of these questions and if you are not prepared to experiment but would like to deviate from the usual, then try the neat growing, upright, broad-leafed 'Handsworthensis'.

Before we leave hedging plants though, we must consider the conifers, for although many are recommended for hedging only the common yew, *Taxus baccata*, has anything to offer the cottage gardener. Most other conifers, apart from being out of context, are screening rather than hedging plants. Never, ever plant that frightful hybrid *Cupressocyparis leylandii* in your cottage garden; it's a rapid growing monster that will soon become an embarrassment.

Preparation and planting of hedges

Selection of the correct hedging subject for your particular soil, location and visual need is only part of the story. Good hedges do not just happen, they originate from careful soil preparation and aftercare. Mark out the site of your hedge and then prepare an area one metre (one yard) wide for the entire length (Fig. 4). If the soil is very heavy and prone to water-logging in the winter, then a tile drain or a trench filled with old brickbats 60 cm (2 ft) or so beneath the surface and leading to a soakaway should be invaluable. A hedge where plants are sitting in the wet will grow in an uneven fashion and be a

Fig 4. Hedge planting.

(*a*) The site of the hedge is dug deeply.

(*b*) Well-rotted manure of leaf mould is forked into the soil.

(*c*) Damaged roots should be trimmed off.

(*d*) Plant between 30 cm and 50 cm (1 ft and 1 ft 8 in) apart depending upon the subject. Firm well in.

constant source of irritation. If the soil is largely composed of sub-soil, as is the case on a recently vacated building site, then incorporate plenty of well-rotted manure, leaf mould or other organic matter. Remember that in the case of a boundary hedge this is the last opportunity of getting down into the soil to enrich it for probably the next forty or fifty years. Dig the designated area thoroughly, removing any perennial weeds, especially creeping weeds like bellbind which enjoy hedgerow conditions and are virtually impossible to eradicate, once well established. Allow the soil to weather, and then break it down into a reasonable tilth before planting.

Hedging subjects can now be planted at almost any time of the year as they are grown and sold in containers. It is generally a bad idea to try and establish a hedge during the summer as you will have all kinds of watering problems to contend with, apart from which the purchase of container grown hedging is inordinately expensive compared with that of bare rooted stock purchased during the dormant season. Deciduous hedging is best planted during the winter, but broadleaved evergreens and conifers should be left until the spring.

Select plants that are well furnished to the ground and go for the smaller sizes as these are more manageable and easier to get established. Large plants seem to provide an instant barrier, but unless you are exceptionally lucky they will tend to have naked lower parts and rarely fill out to make an impenetrable hedge. Plant between 30 cm and 50 cm (1 ft and 1 ft 8 in) apart depending upon the habit of the subject, where space allows in an alternate triangular fashion. Naturally the closer the plants are set the more quickly the hedge will become serviceable. If time is not a serious consideration a good hedge can be made much more economically by spacing plants further apart and feeding them well to encourage rapid growth. Once successfully established, a young hedge requires considerable attention if it is to be an object of beauty in future years. It is always a mistake to let plants grow tall too quickly. Encourage dense bottom growth by keeping them low initially, otherwise they become top-heavy and unwieldy and can only be rectified by drastic pruning.

EVERGREENS AND CONIFERS

Evergreens

Many gardeners consider broad leaved evergreens to be rather dull. While this might be said about dusty laurels and aucubas in shady town gardens, it is not a very fair assessment of the myriad other species that are available. It is not fair to attribute this unfortunate reputation to laurels or aucubas either, for their dull and dusty image has been created by the generally inhospitable conditions under which they are usually forced to live.

Move them to the cottage garden and they are completely different characters. The common aucuba, *Aucuba japonica* 'Variegata' presents attractive glossy foliage on a neatly round shrub, while the cherry laurel, *Prunus laurocerasus*, is rather more vigorous unless clipped. Both are frequently encountered in old country gardens and are clearly in keeping, but I find that they are rather bold and dominating and prefer them in a corner rather than a focal point in the garden. Reliably evergreen and tolerant of almost all soil conditions they are often at their most useful when forming a background to the garden, especially where one side is bounded by trees, for they are the best of the few broadleaved evergreens which are tolerant of shade.

The common holly, *Ilex aquifolium*, has a similar image and is only regarded highly during the Christmas period. Like aucuba and laurel the holly is tolerant of most situations, although it will not prosper on a severely alkaline soil. There are very many cultivars of the common holly, some of which have strong ties with cottage gardens,

Left: Unlikely combinations can make for happy associations. Although the golden cryptomeria is not a typical cottage garden subject, it is completely at home amongst its old fashioned neighbours.

Below: A warm brick wall provides sufficient protection to allow the cottage gardener to be adventurous. Here the lovely *Fremontia californica* has become comfortably established.

others that are rather bizarre and scarcely recognizable as holly.

There is that extraordinary cultivar 'J.C. Van Tol' for example with leaves that are a dark glossy green and almost spineless, its regular crops of red fruits being the only clue that it is a true holly. Or we can go to the other extreme and find 'Ferox' with its viciously spined leaves, an old-fashioned robust sort that I have already recommended for hedging. Its cream and gold blotched forms known as 'Ferox Argentea' and 'Ferox Aurea' look even more fierce. All are male trees and obviously produce no berries. When this is the case I feel that it is always profitable to go for a variegated cultivar. These are able to pollinate the female cultivars in the *I. aquifolium* group and so ensure berries. I see no reason to persist with a dull green male when a variegated holly can be grown.

Try the *I. altaclarensis* cultivar known as 'Golden Queen', despite a name which suggests otherwise, this is a male. Conversely the variety called 'Golden King' is a female. This fruits profusely with bunches of orange-red berries. Another reliable fruiting variegated holly is 'Argentea Pendula'. Not a particularly common kind now, it is worth seeking out for it is the lovely old variety formerly known as 'Perry's Silver Weeping', a popular name which fittingly describes this elegant beauty. *Ilex altaclarensis* is a hybrid in which it is thought our common holly *I. aquifolium* forms a part, an invaluable plant which has yielded two of the best variegated hollies. Both are female, the 'Golden King' to which I have just referred, and 'Silver Sentinel', a neat upright character with green leaves conspicuously edged with cream.

The hollies provide colour and backbone to the garden during the dull and dreary days of winter and I feel that no sizeable cottage garden can afford to be without at least one. Not so the next evergreen, for I suppose that strictly speaking it is not a cottage-garden plant, although its habit lends itself readily to this art. I am referring to *Garrya elliptica*, that amiable Californian native which displays long grey-green catkins during the depths of winter giving us hope that spring is really only just around the corner. With its dark evergreen foliage and free and easy disposition it should find its way into every garden. Not only does it produce its catkins at an opportune season of the year, but actually enjoys growing in those awkward north-facing situations.

The various elaeagnus species are also known for their lusty growth and handsome foliage, often produced in the face of adversity. Again not widely associated with cottage gardens of the traditional kind, they do fit in well and should be a part of the modern scene. Particularly *Elaeagnus ebbingei*, a substantial, quick growing shrub with large silvery grey leaves that provide a superb foil for the soft blue and pink pastel shades of many of our old fashioned herbaceous perennials. *Elaeagnus oleaster*, the common oleaster, is not as frequently encountered as hitherto. Although with a true claim to cottage garden fame, this large spiny shrub with long and rather narrow silvery-grey foliage has largely been ousted by the Japanese *E. pungens* and its hideous green and gold cultivar 'Maculata'. The last is very brash and vulgar and totally unsuited to the concept that we have in mind.

Conifers

It cannot be said that conifers played a vital role in the cottage gardens of the past, except for perhaps yew and pine. However, that is not to say that they cannot be included now if chosen with care. We must not exclude plants merely because they were not widely cultivated when the cottage garden was in vogue. The sensible gardener will wish to use everything that is suitable and at his disposal, and there is a tremendous diversity of form and colour available to those who contemplate planting conifers in their garden. This wide range of material not only embraces those species and cultivars which are sufficiently modest to be able to reach maturity in the garden, but also

Even when a tree has passed its useful life it can be used to support a
scrambling rose to great effect.

trees which we might more readily associate with the forester.

I am always surprised by the scant attention that we pay our taller growing timber trees. Obviously they are much too vigorous to be incorporated in any long term garden design, but many are attractive in their juvenile state and can be a real asset to the garden in its formative life. The Colorado white fir, *Abies concolor*, is an excellent example. A bold upright tree with a broad sweeping skirt of grey-green foliage. Under garden conditions the life of such a tree is very restricted (say, 10–15 years), but the years of pleasure that it provides more than compensate for the moment of agony when it has to be felled. Of course purists will disagree with such a practice and doggedly advocate the use of conifers which will not outgrow their positions. Those who follow this belief and want a fir in their garden will have to be content with *Abies koreana*.

The majority of gardeners associate conifers with the Lawson's cypress *Chamaecyparis lawsoniana*, the usual but variable upright growing conifer with green foliage which appears in most modern gardens. Not always in its original form, but often as different named cultivars of almost every shape, size and hue imaginable. There is the slow growing, columnar grey-green 'Ellwoodii' and its nearly indistinguishable cousin 'Fletcheri' as well as the vigorous green 'Erecta Viridis', 'Kilmacurragh' and 'Pottenii'. There are the rich golden-yellow cultivars 'Stewartii' and 'Golden King' as well as the incomparable steely-blue 'Allumii'. All are excellent garden plants and each has at least one lesser known counterpart of equal merit which deserves much wider plantings; cultivars like 'Green Hedger' and 'Winston Churchill' for example.

With the former it is probably the unfortunate name that has led to this lack of popularity, for although first class for screening it is also a very good specimen conifer. Of dense habit, it is liberally clothed with splendid rich green foliage. 'Winston Churchill' on the other hand cannot blame its lack of popularity upon its name. Nor can any fault be found with its broad columnar habit or bright golden foliage. The reason that this cultivar has not replaced either 'Stewartii' or 'Golden King' in modern gardens is quite baffling, for it is without doubt the best golden chamaecyparis of all.

Not all the best cultivars are medium or tall growing, for *C. lawsoniana* has sired a number of very fine dwarf conifers as well – splendid little fellows like 'Minima Glauca' and 'Forsteckensis'. Both of these are slow growing and ultimately form dense globular bushes. The foliage of 'Forsteckensis' being congested and much divided, while that of 'Minima Glauca' is produced in neat upright sprays arranged in much the same manner as the pages of a book. These are a rich green with just a tinge of blue, whereas the foliage of 'Forsteckensis' is dull green and devoid of any lustre.

Dwarf and slow growing forms are abundant amongst the thujas, the majority being derived from the American arbor vitae; *Thuja occidentalis* 'Rheingold' is undoubtedly the best of these. A rich golden mound of foliage with a coppery flush during the winter. It can be rather variable, some plants exhibiting a rather coarse and open habit while others display fine feathery foliage which grows into a neat tight ball. The Chinese arbor-vitae, *T. orientalis* has also given rise to several slow growing cultivars, notable amongst these being 'Rosedalis'. This is a strange little conifer which makes a rounded bush of blue-green foliage flushed with the golden-green of young growth in spring, but turning pinkish-purple during the winter. 'Cuprea' which is derived from *T. plicata*, also has variable coloration, the entire bush sparkling with golden-yellow juvenile foliage.

Thuja plicata has also given us the delightful little 'Rogersii'. This is a very slow growing pyramidal form with crowded foliage of bronze and gold. A first class dwarf, it does appreciate protection from searing winds or scorching sun as its new growth is rather tender and vulnerable to burning. Of

Arising from amongst the tangled informality of the border, this rose
provides an eye-catching focal point.

course the parent of this little beauty, *T. plicata*, is itself very resilient, only suffering in the very occasional harsh winters that we have to endure. A native of western North America, it is popularly known as western red cedar and will ultimately attain quite a size. It has a handsome pyramidal outline when grown as a specimen and possesses the most agreeable fruity aroma which is enhanced if you run your fingers through the foliage on a warm summer's day.

FLOWERING SHRUBS

Most of the flowering shrubs which we lovingly cultivate have their origins in the cottage garden. Unfortunately few have retained the charm of former years, plant breeders having worked upon old favourites and turned them into bigger, better and more colourful characters with greater disease tolerance. Often scent has been lost in the process, but if we are realistic we must admit that much of what we have now is far superior in decorative terms to that enjoyed by our grandparents. A careful ramble through the nurseryman's catalogue still presents us with the opportunity of recreating a cottage garden atmosphere with plants that are not too far removed from those of the period. Indeed, the wealth available makes selection difficult, so I am basing my own selection upon those that evoke memories for me of my grandmother's garden – a garden on heavy clay soil in the wind-swept East Anglian countryside, where the art of cottage gardening flourished.

Lilacs and forsythia

Lilacs were amongst the most successful, particularly cultivars of the common *Syringa vulgaris*. The named progeny of this rather mundane species runs into hundreds, varying in colour from white, through pale pink and mauve to deep rose and purple, with either single or double blossoms. 'Souvenir de Louis Spaeth' is probably the best loved of the single kinds. A bold fellow with blossoms of deep port wine in dense conical panicles. The snow-white 'Maud Notcutt' is one of the best recent introductions and 'Primrose' one of the most unusual.

Of the double lilacs 'Charles Joly' reigns supreme, an excellent dark purple cultivar which flowers slightly later than most other kinds. The creamy-white 'Madame Lemoine' is equally well known and together with the soft lilac-pink 'Belle de Nancy' completes a trio of really dependable garden shrubs. As I intimated earlier, the ordinary *S. vulgaris* is rather gloomy, but its white form *alba* is still encountered in older gardens and has a special charm of its own. It may not be quite so floriferous as the modern cultivars, but it is a solid and dependable character.

There is another important group of lilacs that are not strictly speaking cottage garden shrubs, but which are ideal for the cottage garden. These are popularly called Canadian hybrids following their development at a research station in Ottawa in the 1920s by a Miss Isabella Preston. They are amazingly resilient plants, growing into sizeable bushes which during early summer froth and foam with pendent panicles of colourful blossoms. There are so many hybrids that you are spoiled for choice, but I like the deep pink 'Audrey' and immense purplish-pink 'Isabella'.

The forsythia, its boughs laden with delicate golden bells is a regular harbinger of spring and as inextricably tied up with the cottage garden as the lilac. *Forsythia intermedia* 'Spectabilis' is the one usually grown and most frequently sold prepacked by the chain stores. That is not to imply that it is in any way inferior, but more recent introductions like 'Beatrix Farrand' and 'Lynwood Gold' do produce larger blossoms of a more intense hue. For those with limited space, *F. ovata* can be recommended. A neat bush no more than 1·5 m (5 ft) high, its naked branches are sprinkled evenly with bright yellow blossoms.

The most prolific of the species is *F. suspensa*, a large pendulous shrub of lax and untidy growth which is seen at its best when grown against a wall, although some gardeners use it as ground cover. If you have an awkward bank to disguise it is especially useful. Plant it towards the top and peg its main branches down (Fig. 5) and it will soon become an impenetrable mass, turning into

Fig 5. Layering.

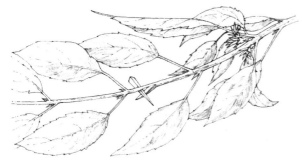

(*a*) An incision is made in an unflowered lateral shoot at a point where it will conveniently touch the ground. The cut is held apart.

(*b*) The shoot is pegged to the soil by a piece of bent wire or a large staple.

a tumbling cascade of gold during early spring. Forsythias illuminate the spring garden. Give them a dark background of evergreens or plant them in association with bright red flowering currants like *Ribes sanguineum* 'King Edward VII'. The shorter growing kinds can be interplanted with the lilac-purple *Rhododendron* 'Praecox', while those that are used for ground cover benefit from a generous sprinkling of blue grape hyacinths or muscari in their midst.

Potentillas, hypericums and periwinkles

What the forsythias do for the spring, the potentillas do for the summer, especially the shrubby types like *Potentilla dahurica* and *P. fruticosa*. It is not the parents that are of great interest, but their progeny, like the pure white 'Abbotswood' and its contemporary 'Mount Everest', both derived from the short compact *P. dahurica*. Cultivars of *P. fruticosa* tend to be larger and more rangy, witness the two popular yellow cultivars 'Katherine Dykes' and 'Moonlight'. 'Tangerine' is an excellent orange-yellow which stands alone, together with the rich yellow 'Elizabeth'. No mention of potentillas would be complete without 'Red Ace', a controversial plant which has gained tremendous publicity for potentillas both favourable and ill. When growing in a situation to its liking it is quite outstanding, but I have equally seen it looking washed out and sad. However, the lovely rich carmine-pink 'Royal Flush' looks to be stealing its thunder and is likely to be the potentilla of the future.

Alongside potentillas I would place hypericums as plants for the summer. Not only the common rose of sharon, *Hypericum calycinum*, but many lesser known kinds, especially the named varieties. One of the best of these is 'Elstead', a cultivar derived from *H. inodorum* with small flowers and spectacular fruits. The soft yellow blossoms are produced in terminal clusters and followed by the most brilliant salmon-red berries. *Hypericum androsaemum* is of similar habit with golden flowers and glossy black fruits. The cultivar 'Hidcote' provides the largest flowers of any of the hypericums. Of indeterminate origin, this has spreading saucer-shaped blossoms of rich golden-yellow which smother the plant from late summer until early autumn. Unlike most hypericums it forms a compact bush scarcely 1·5 m (5 ft) high. *Hypericum moseranum* is smaller still, a compact ground hugging plant with attractive fresh green leaves and myriad bright yellow flowers.

I am not sure whether periwinkles are shrubs or not, but they are of a persistent nature and more or less evergreen. They are also exceedingly useful, flourishing in dark dry corners where nothing else will grow. Here they produce starry blossoms of blue, white or maroon with a frequency that seems to be directly proportional to the harshness of the conditions that they are compelled to endure. The lesser periwinkle, *Vinca minor*, and greater periwinkle, *V. major*, are those that adorned cottage gardens in years gone by, together with cultivars like 'Alba' and 'Burgundy', and the double flowered 'Multiplex'. All flower from late spring until mid-summer amongst handsome dark green foliage.

However, it is not one of these that I favour, but the soft blue *V. difformis*, a well behaved native of southern Europe which, if given a little shelter, will flower continuously from late autumn until early summer. The inward glow and feeling of wonder engendered by just a glimpse of its starry blossoms peeping through the winter snow would be ample justification for its inclusion in my garden.

Daphne and Rubus

So would the scent of the daphnes, for these are amongst the finest fragrant shrubs for the small garden. Few cottage gardens do not accommodate at least one plant of our native mezereon, *Daphne mezereum*. During late winter and early spring the naked branches of this elegant little shrub are wreathed in blossoms of rich reddish-purple, followed by vivid scarlet berries. Unfortunately it is not a long-lived shrub and therefore requires regular replacement. Luckily it produces viable seed in abundance which, if sown immediately it ripens, germinates freely. Seedlings must be pot grown as they resent root disturbance and do not transplant successfully from open ground.

Some of the decorative brambles will tolerate a bit of shade, but usually fare better in the open. Brambles are not usually thought of as desirable garden plants as the wild thorny species have given them a bad name. This is unfortunate, for the genus *Rubus* as a whole embraces some of the most

interesting shrubs for the informal garden. Of course some are conventional and thorny, like the white-washed brambles. These are species of modest growth with stems of glistening white. Where space can be found they present a picture of stark beauty, their naked white stems sparkling in the winter sunshine against a backdrop of dark evergreens. *Rubus biflorus* and *R. cockburnianus* are the usual ones grown, easy-going characters that ask for little more than an open position and the annual removal of canes.

Other flowering shrubs

There are so many other shrubs that I could describe that would enhance a cottage garden. Mock oranges or philadelphus with their fragrant summer blossoms of cream and white. Various brooms in every shape, size and hue imaginable. Some like the Mount Etna broom, *Genista aetnensis* erupt into a great fountain of gold, others like *Cytisus kewensis* create tumbling creamy cascades. There are the winter flowering viburnums, *V. farreri* and *V. bodnantense*, with fragrant flowers of cream and pink. The common laurustinus, *V. tinus*, sporting pinkish-white clusters of tiny blossoms amongst handsome dark evergreen foliage. The witch hazel, *Hamamelis mollis*, its branches outstretched and revealing fragrant red and gold blossoms during mid-winter.

Every season has its possibilities and some of these I have noted. Get out into the countryside and see what other gardeners are doing. It is even better to visit private gardens that are open to the public for charity, especially those belonging to small suburban gardeners.

A REVIEW OF THE ROSES

No cottage garden can be considered complete without its complement of roses. Not the roses of the modern day with their iridescent colours and feeble scents, but the

Everyone's idea of the perfect cottage garden, with roses around the door.
With a little care this can become reality.

bold old fashioned shrub roses that were all the rage just before the turn of the century. Although many suffered a decline in popularity after the First World War, in recent years they have made a come-back and are now more readily available.

One of the oldest roses and the one with which I associate cottage gardens is the moss rose, *Rosa centifolia* 'Muscosa', named for the reddish-green moss on the flower buds. The blossoms are soft delicate pink, fully double and possess a spicy fragrance that announces 'cottage garden' to the world. Like all the old roses it prefers a soil that is on the heavy side, but is not fussy as to whether this is of acid or alkaline persuasion. A sunny position is essential well away from the drip of overhanging trees which can cause the balling and browning of blossoms. A vigorous grower, I can remember this particular rose invading the elderly hawthorn hedge in my grandmother's cottage garden. In mid-summer it cheekily waved fresh wands of foliage above its support, each garlanded in pink cabbagy blossoms. Despite attempts to curb its activities, it became inextricably bound up with the hawthorn and there it remains to this day.

The gallica roses are the parents of the modern rose and had a big part to play in the development of the moss rose. *Rosa gallica* itself is known as the French rose, and more importantly its cultivar the old red damask, *R. gallica* 'Officinalis' as the apothecary's rose. It was this latter that was thought during the Middle Ages to be able to provide a cure for almost every known human ailment. *Rosa gallica* is a rather lax shrub, scarcely ever more than 1·5 m (5 ft) high with saucer-like pink blossoms which are followed by bold, rounded, brick-red hips. Its partner, 'Officinalis' is of similar habit, but with fragrant, semi-double, rosy-crimson flowers. There is also an old cottage garden rose popularly referred to as 'Rosa mundi', but really *R. gallica* 'Versicolor', which occurred as a branch sport from the apothecary's rose and has semi-double flowers that are striped with red and white.

Damask roses are derived from *R. damascena*, a short shrubby character with large clusters of red, pink or white richly fragrant flowers and vicious thorny stems. They are ancient roses of mixed parentage, believed to be old hybrids rather than true species, but so old that their origins are lost in the mists of time. There are innumerable named cultivars in modern catalogues, but for interest and cottage garden authenticity I would select the double soft pink 'Trigintipetala', an old kind that is used in the production of attar of roses.

Climbing and rambling roses are discussed in Chapter 4, so they find no place here, but the diversity that remains is still overwhelming. Those just mentioned would be a must in my cottage garden, but there are others that are worthy contenders and to which I must introduce you. Relatives of the moss rose, like its progenitor, the cabbage rose, *R. centifolia*; with both fragrant flowers and foliage it is an absolute delight. There is the dainty China rose, *R. chinensis*, the forerunner of the delightful fairy roses typified by *R. chinensis* 'Minima'. We have sweet briars, *R. rubiginosa*, that can be utilized as a hedge and the ramanas rose, *R. rugosa*, which is equally at home in a difficult corner. This boisterous fellow has yielded many fine cultivars, amongst which the pale rose-pink 'Frau Dagmar Hastrup' reigns supreme. Not only are the blossoms lovely, but so too are the rich crimson hips. And there are dwarf burnet roses derived from *R. pimpinellifolia*, which make low thickets of thorny branches thronged during early summer with tiny sweetly scented blossoms.

Roses with cottage garden associations are nearly as many as the pebbles on the beach. If you are unsure about what you require, then visit one of the very many good collections that are growing in gardens open to the public and judge for yourself. Mid-summer is the time to check out the flowers, but many have useful and decorative fruits too and these should be looked at again during early autumn.

3

FRUIT, FOLIAGE AND BARK

Fruit, foliage and bark are important but often neglected considerations in the garden. In traditional cottage gardens they were very necessary additions, especially the fruiting species which provided the raw material for jams, preserves and drinks. Even though we have a more restricted space nowadays, we have a much better choice than our grandparents, so few modern gardens of the cottage style have any excuse for excluding a small tree. Of course, great care is necessary when selecting a tree, especially if you have a tiny garden, for it is going to remain in the same position for many years and therefore must conform with its surroundings. Remember that young trees are like puppies – they grow up! It always saddens me to see forest trees which have been planted in small gardens butchered with a chain saw to keep them within bounds. How much better it is to grow a tree that will fill its designated space naturally.

ORNAMENTAL TREES

Sorbus family

Of all the trees that one would consider for a cottage garden, those of the *Sorbus* family contain the widest diversity and are the most appropriate. The family is divided into groups, two of the major ones being headed by trees that are native to Britain. *Sorbus aucuparia* heads the *aucuparia* section and is the rowan or mountain ash, an important tree for the cottage garden in Scotland where traditionally it is planted to keep away witches and demons. The whitebeam *S. aria* is the most important species in the *aria* section. Members of the *aucuparia*

group have pinnate leaves with numerous leaflets, while those in the *aria* division have simple, toothed or lobed leaves, often with an attractive greyish bloom. Our native mountain ash, *S. aucuparia*, is an excellent tree in its own right, with fresh green pinnately divided leaves, bold clusters of creamy-white blossoms, and large bunches of orange or red fruits that can be converted into the most delicious rowan jelly. It can be a little overpowering in the smaller garden, where it is generally better replaced by the similar, but upright growing 'Sheerwater Seedling'.

The laciniate rowan, *S. aucuparia* 'Asplenifolia' is an elegant tree with deeply cut fern-like foliage, while *S. a.* 'Xanthocarpa' has fruits of rich orange-yellow. 'Joseph Rock' is an *aucuparia* type of uncertain origin, which in addition to having creamy-yellow fruits produces the most magnificent crimson-purple autumn foliage. *Sorbus scalaris* is a rather spreading species with dense flat clusters of small red fruits, a contrast to *S. discolor* which has a bold, upright, vase-shaped crown, during autumn heavily laden with bunches of orange-red fruits that sparkle amongst its fiery foliage.

The whitebeams consist mostly of our native *S. aria* and its progeny. Although a common and widespread inhabitant of chalk downlands in southern Britain, it is not a tree to be passed over, for it has an attractive compact dome-shaped head of grey-green foliage and bold clusters of deep red, waxy fruits. Some of its progeny are a little more refined, but I do not necessarily think that this renders them superior in the cottage garden. The much talked about golden-leafed *S. aria* 'Chrysophylla' has magnificent foliage, but a less pleasing habit, while the pendulous *S. a.* 'Pendula' provides a useful shape but precious little else.

Sorbus aria 'Decaisneana' which is known to older cottage gardeners as 'Majestica', is the prince of the whitebeams, having expansive grey-green leaves and yielding substantial clusters of large red fruits. The aptly named *S. a.* 'Lutescens' produces leaves coated on the upper surfaces with creamygold down, while the hybrid *S. thuringiaca* is blessed with leaves that have a thick grey tomentum beneath. A hybrid between the rowan and the whitebeam, this little fellow is especially useful, having a good upright habit that is best seen in the selection offered by nurserymen as *S. t.* 'Fastigiata'. Of all the fastigiate trees, this is the least offensive, having a columnar habit in which the branches ascend in an easy fashion.

Cherry family

Most fastigiate trees look as if they have been tortured, possessing a stiff unnatural habit in which the foliage often appears less than typical of the original species. This is particularly evident in those derived from forest trees. I think that trees that are naturally of modest proportions are preferable, and for these we need look no further than the cherry family. Not just flowering cherries, which are a part of any cottage garden, but those that have other virtues to be treasured as well. *Prunus serrula* is one of the most remarkable, with an incredible bark like polished red-brown mahogany. Against a clear blue sky and a backdrop of snow this provides one of the most spectacular sights in the garden on a winter day. It flowers as well with tiny white blossoms like delicate snowflakes sprinkled amongst its willowy branches. Attractive bark is a virtue of *P. sargentii* as well, together with myriad pink blossoms and the richest orange-red autumn colour one could imagine.

Decorative cherries grow well on rich heavy soils, especially those of an alkaline persuasion. Species and cultivars that are grown for their decorative blossoms and those that are cultivated for the pleasure of their decorative bark should be grown as half-standards or standards; that is they should have a clear length of stem. Others, like the autumn flowering *P. subhirtella autumnalis* are easier to manage when grown as a bush.

Maples

Maples are important trees for providing autumn foliage colour and decorative winter bark. The most popular for small gardens are the Japanese maples, *Acer palmatum* and its progeny, although it should be remembered that they will only prosper on an acid or neutral soil. *Acer palmatum* is rarely planted in its original form, which is a pity as its soft green leaves and low easy charm are just what is required in a cottage garden. The purple-leafed cultivar 'Atropurpureum' is the closest that we can usually get, and if carefully placed this does nearly as well. The *palmatum* group of Japanese maples have typical five or seven lobed leaves which are much more divided in the *dissectum* group. Cultivars in this section are usually much smaller and tend to form mushroom-shaped shrubs rather than trees. This tends to give them an oriental look which is not always easy to accommodate in a traditional cottage garden.

UTILITY PLANTS: FRUITS AND NUTS

While the subject of this book is the decorative cottage garden, it is important not to overlook utility plants. Many utility plants can fulfil all our decorative requirements, and yield a useful harvest as well. For example, take some of the odd nuts and fruits which make an unexpected, but welcome addition to the garden. It is only in the cottage garden that the cultivation of some of these can be really justified.

Medlar

I am thinking now of the medlar, *Mespilus germanica*, an easily grown fruit of unusual

The striking *Acer pseudoplatanus* 'Brilliantissimum' will eventually soften
the skyline and give the garden much needed height.

taste and appearance borne on a tree with a quaint gnarled 'old man' look about it. With bright green foliage and white or pinkish tinged flowers, it is a considerable asset to the olde worlde garden. If one is a purist about these things, it can be treated as an apple in all respects, although I prefer to leave it alone except for the removal of untidy branches. The fruits form during summer and should be allowed to hang on the tree until late autumn, after which they can be spread out in a cool airy place until bletted. This really means that the fruits are starting to decay, and it is at this time that they are ready for eating or converting into wine or jelly. The taste for medlars is an acquired one, but if you are really interested in producing fruit rather than considering the tree purely as decorative, then get the cultivar 'The Nottingham'. This is often available as a standard or half standard grafted on to a pear, hawthorn or quince rootstock.

Quince

The quince, *Cydonia oblonga*, and the medlar are closely related and desire similar garden conditions, except that the fruits of the quince are used when ripe and should not be picked until they are fully mature. A number of kinds are in cultivation, all excellent decorative trees, but not always easy to come by. The Portugal quince is the most likely to be encountered and is the best sort for cooking and preserving. The apple and pear-shaped cultivars differ only in shape and keeping quality, while 'Bereczki' is well thought of by those with a delicate palate. The quince is a handsome spreading tree with broad green leaves, white spring blossom, and lovely grey bark. An easy going character for which I have a strong affection.

Peaches, apricots and nectarines

I also like to see a peach or apricot in the cottage garden. Usually a hit and miss affair outdoors when it comes to fruit, they are very much a part of old cottage gardens where they can still be seen clothing southerly or westerly walls. Fruit is anyway a secondary consideration when they are grown outside, it is for the sparkling pink blossoms that bedeck their naked branches in early spring that most cottagers grow them. If a peach or two can be secured this is an added bonus, but not a major consideration.

The number of cultivars available that have any prospect of flourishing outside are somewhat limited, especially amongst the apricots. 'Moorpark' is the easiest to get hold of, a large rounded, yellowish fruit with one side a reddish-brown colour. It is seldom ripe before early autumn, so if you hope for something earlier then try 'Early Moorpark'. Peach cultivars are more abundant, the American 'Amsden June' being the earliest while the handsome large fruited 'Duke of York' runs it a close second. The best known of all though, is 'Peregrine', a late summer kind with medium-sized fruit of excellent quality. We must not forget nectarines, a sort of smooth skinned peach amongst which 'Early Rivers' and 'Lord Napier' are the most common.

The cultivation of peaches, nectarines and apricots in the cottage garden is very similar. Remember that if you seek fruit, and indeed flower, that apricots bear fruit on spurs as well as on young wood. This means that when pruning apricots, unwanted laterals should be cut back to two buds instead of being removed altogether. All three kinds enjoy life on a sunny wall in an alkaline soil.

Of course it would be easy to justify the inclusion of apples, pears, cherries, plums and other top fruits here because they often form an integral part of the cottage garden and have been traditionally planted in the ornamental part. However, I think that I have probably gone down the road as far as I can with fruits of culinary value, that is unless you include the nuts. There are innumerable nuts that can be grown in the garden, but the most appropriate are the cobs and filberts.

Native trees, like the common silver birch are reliable and hardy,
providing instant maturity to the freshly established garden.

Cob nuts and hazel nuts

The cob nut is the type in which the outer husk is very short, while the filbert has a longer outer husk which totally enfolds it. Several cultivars are available, amongst them 'Cannon Ball', 'Cosford' and 'Kentish Cob'. Nuts will grow in almost any soil, but a free-draining loam is ideal. They grow well in the shade and can be interplanted with other shrubs in a border, but at least two different varieties should be grown to ensure adequate pollination. Nuts are rather different from other fruiting plants in that they produce both male and female catkins which are pollinated by the wind. These appear before the foliage, and once their work is done, the bushes can be pruned so that just enough nut-bearing wood remains to give an acceptable crop.

The bushes should be encouraged to develop an urn-shaped framework, the leading growths being shortened and thinned. Wood that carried a crop the previous year must be spurred back. Occasionally wands or suckers spring up from the roots and these should be torn away. Nuts are ready to harvest during early autumn, just as the foliage is turning a lovely butter-yellow. After picking, spread them out in trays in a cool, well-ventilated building. They will be ready for use during the winter.

The nuts also have amongst their number several varieties that are grown exclusively for foliage colour. The golden-leafed hazel nut, *Corylus avellana* 'Aurea' has golden leaves throughout the year, but I am afraid that I cannot get too excited about this as it needs very careful placing in partial shade if leaf scorch is to be avoided. This does not happen with *C. maxima* 'Purpurea' which sports handsome purplish leaves on an upright shrub of stately aspect. This is lovely next to the pendulous willow-leafed pear, *Pyrus salicifolia* 'Pendula' which forms a round topped small tree clothed in a tumbling cascade of silver-grey foliage. One of the best of the silver or grey-leaved subjects for the cottage garden and one of the few that is reliably hardy.

FOLIAGE COLOUR

Most foliage colour in a cottage garden has to be provided by autumn subjects. Otherwise it is difficult to get happy blends and associations. Strongly variegated trees and shrubs are alien to our concept and some of the brighter yellow and purple foliage subjects are equally tasteless.

The stagshorn sumach, *Rhus typhina*, is a splendid example of what we should look for. An easy going small tree or shrub with large pinnate leaves which turn vivid orange and red in the autumn, each branch crowned with contrasting conical deep red-brown clusters of fruits. A suckering subject, this should be planted on poor soil in an out of the way place where it can sucker freely and provide a colourful background for choicer subjects.

The elderberries are similar propositions; for although highly decorative, they are a bit coarse for the more intimate garden and make a better background than focal point. Most of the green-leaved kinds turn yellow during the autumn, but the purple-leaved *Sambucus nigra* 'Purpurea' and much-divided fern-leaved elder, *S. n.* 'Laciniata' are excellent throughout the summer as well.

Crab apples can aso provide useful summer leaf colour, although traditionally thought of as autumn foliage and fruiting subjects. The hybrid *Malus purpurea* is one of the best all round kinds with dark purplish-green foliage and during spring, rosy-crimson flowers. The small apple-like fruits are light crimson-purple and very similar to those of the well known 'Profusion'. In many ways this remarkable cultivar is superior to the straightforward hybrid, sporting coppery-crimson leaves and wine-red flowers. Be careful how you use it though, as in some gardens it could look a little brash. I would also be cautious about the use of other first class kinds like 'Golden Hornet' and 'Red Sentinel'. They are so good that in the cottage garden they appear too good to be true and then are out of keeping.

Although not commonly associated with cottage gardens, the golden
gleditsia can add brightness and charm to the cottage garden. Difficult to
establish, it prefers sheltered sites.

35

Fig 6. Tree planting.

(*a*) Digging the hole.

(*b*) A peat mixture is incorporated.

(*c*) The tree is placed in position adjacent the stake.

(*d*) The tree is removed and stake is knocked in.

(*e*) The tree is repositioned in the hole.

(*f*) The hole re-filled with soil. Secure fastening of the tree to the stake is by means of a tree tie.

Few early cottagers would have expected a third of the yield of fruits provided by 'Golden Hornet'. But it would not have been this crab that they would have favoured. The crab apples of cottage gardens always had to yield useful fruits as well as provide decoration and in many cases this would have been that old stalwart 'John Downie', a lovely little tree that is as popular now as it was at the end of the last century. Of small neat habit, it has typical apple foliage, white blossoms and gorgeous, large, conical, orange and red fruits that make a fine jelly.

PREPARATION AND PLANTING FOR TREES AND SHRUBS

Trees and shrubs should be planted as early as possible in the development of the garden so that they can be growing while the rest of the operations are going on. They can be planted at any time during their dormancy period, which extends from autumn through to early spring. Garden centres offer trees and shrubs in containers for planting during the summer months, but these need careful maintenance after planting. With trees especially, I would hesitate about their purchase in containers unless their foliage is bright and green and the roots not pot-bound. The ground that they are to occupy should be well prepared as it must be remembered that each tree or shrub will occupy the same piece of land for many years to come. I prefer planting to take place

during the autumn, for the soil will not have become cold and the tree or shrub has an opportunity to make some root growth before the winter sets in. Late planting causes all kinds of problems as the ground is cold and the bitter winds of early spring shrivel the emerging buds and hamper growth.

All that is required for planting is a hole of sufficient size to accommodate all the roots without cramping them (Fig. 6). It should also be of sufficient depth to allow the shrub or tree to settle to where it was in the nursery row. This can be quite clearly determined by looking for the stain at the base of the trunk or main stem caused by the previous soil level. Any damaged or broken roots should be trimmed back with secateurs and the plant stood in the hole. If it is a tree that will require a stake, then this is knocked in before the hole is filled so that damage to the roots does not occur. The hole is filled with crumbly soil, the tree or shrub being worked up and down so that all the nooks and crannies between the roots are filled with particles and no troublesome air pockets occur.

The soil surface is then firmed down and if it is a tree that has been planted, then this is attached to a stake with proper tree ties, or else with a short length of garden hose through which twine is threaded, the hose preventing the stake, tree and twine from rubbing one another when tied. In country districts where rabbits may be troublesome, wire netting, sacking or specially manufactured tape can be wrapped around the trunks to prevent the bark being stripped.

4

CLIMBERS AND SCRAMBLERS

Climbing and scrambling plants are those that depend upon another for support. In the wild they often grow in hedgerows or amongst the understorey of deciduous woodlands. In the tropics they scramble into trees, growing quickly in their search for light. This gives us a clue as to their cultural requirements, for they enjoy their heads in the sunshine, their roots in cool shade. It is not an indisputable rule, but one that applies to the greater number of plants under discussion here. It is certainly a requirement of clematis, for these are naturally hedgerow plants and to be grown successfully require a cool root run, yet their foliage and flowers benefit from maximum sunlight. This can be contrived by planting small shrubs like potentilla around the base of a plant, or else putting a paving slab on top of the soil close by the roots. It is important not to pave so close to the roots that the free passage of moisture is impeded.

Clematis

Clematis are regarded by most gardeners as the queen of the climbers and justifiably so. This diverse genus, which includes a few non-climbing species too, has a range of colour, form and flowering period unequalled by any other group of climbers. The diversity of clematis is such that they can be used in almost any role. Modern hybrids are excellent for clothing walls and fences. Species like *Clematis montana* will happily festoon an old fruit tree or cover an outhouse, while the non-clinging *C. durandii* will trail as well as scramble.

However, for the majority of gardeners it is the large flowered cultivars that hold the greatest attraction. Bold starry blossoms in almost every colour imaginable and in varie-

ties that will start flowering during early spring and carry on until late summer. There are two of these that are widely grown and loved by all gardeners, 'Jackmanii Superba' and 'Nelly Moser'. The first named flowers during mid-summer with deep purple flowers, while 'Nelly Moser' is more refined with a somewhat extended flowering season during which it produces beautifully sculptured blossoms of rich mauve with a conspicuous lilac bar. 'Ville de Lyon' is carmine red and 'Duchess of Edinburgh' has double flowers of milky-white, while 'Ernest Markham' is rich magenta. 'Lincoln Star' has raspberry-pink flowers, 'Richard Pennell' blossoms of deepest lavender, whereas those of 'Proteus' are lilac-rose and fully double, like an old-fashioned paeony.

The spring-blooming *C. montana* is the most popular of the species and the one with the greatest cottage garden appeal. An easy-going plant of vigorous habit with myriad small creamy-white blossoms. There are several forms and cultivars, including the pink-flowered *rubens*, rich rose-pink 'Tetrarose' and fragrant, soft pink 'Elizabeth'. These are all boisterous climbers that benefit from having their main stems tied to their host for support to prevent them being blown down in high winds. Unlike the large flowered hybrids that require a strict pruning regime, *C. montana* and its progeny are merely tidied up each year and kept within bounds.

The pruning of clematis is a much discussed subject, but in very general terms can be simplified. With large flowered hybrids, it is a question of pruning early flowering cultivars down to the ground after flowering. This enables them to produce

38

Left: A kaleidoscope of colour in the mixed border. Aquilegias and geraniums tumble about, while the rose 'Maigold' provides a colourful backdrop.

Below: This walled enclosure gives an opportunity to establish climbing subjects like the beautiful golden hop, *Humulus lupulus* 'Aureus'.

Wisteria and climbing roses are typical of the cottage garden, giving it
atmosphere and providing a colourful foil for other plants.

wood during the summer that will then yield blossoms the following year. Those that do not come into bloom until well into the summer flower on the current season's growth. Therefore these need cutting to the ground during early spring.

Most species, although being given a definite pruning sequence in gardening books, in practice are left to their own devices. Just keep them within bounds and remove dead, dying or weak growths. As the majority of gardeners grow their species clematis amongst shrubs, this is an easy and natural way of doing things. The only exception that I would make is the lemon peel clematis, *C. orientalis*. This is really much better if cut to the ground each spring. For the late summer this clematis is exceptional, producing its strange yellow flowers until the first sharp autumn frosts and following them with attractive silky seed heads that often persist into the winter creating a stark but beautiful sight when covered with hoarfrost or a dusting of snow. *Clematis tangutica* is another yellow-flowered species, but one which scarcely looks like a clematis. Its nodding blossoms are produced in abundance during mid-summer and are followed by beautiful spidery seed heads which are as soft as silk.

Innumerable other clematis deserve a place in the cottage garden, but none more so than *C. cirrhosa*. Given a sheltered corner facing west or south this splendid evergreen will produce its creamy-green flowers during early spring. It is a shy blooming plant in its formative life, but once established in a situation to its liking will cheer the gardener every spring with its delicate blossoms.

While there are exceptions, most clematis are equally at home on the house wall or scrambling freely amongst trees and shrubs. The selection of the variety to grow is purely a matter of personal taste. Success with clematis and all other climbers is dependent upon correct planting rather than any other factor. Climbers planted next to a wall will often have to contend with dry and

dusty conditions where the soil is overhung by the eaves of the roof. Concrete wall foundations will interfere with root development as well. It is important to plant in a position that allows the climber to proceed to its support unimpeded, yet provides for amenable soil conditions (Fig. 7a).

Fig 7. Planting clematis.

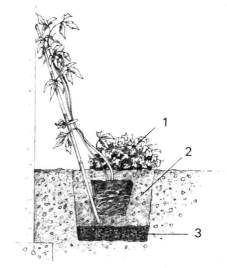

(a) When planting against a wall take care to avoid dry hostile conditions. 1. The clematis roots should be shaded by a small plant. 2. A mixture of loam and peat with bonemeal added. 3. Good garden compost.

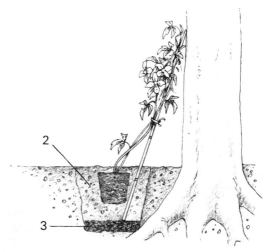

(b) When planting against a tree try to avoid the roots. A cane should be used for support until the vigorous young shoots reach their support.

When the soil is very dry a generous quantity of peat should be incorporated to retain moisture and aid initial establishment. Root interference is a problem that also arises when a climber is planted near the base of a tree. During the summer the leaf canopy effectively keeps moisture from the roots of the newly planted climber too, so great care must be taken in selecting the planting site. It is much better to plant a climber or scrambler 60–75 cm (2–2½ ft) from its support and trail the initial growths along the ground rather than try to establish it in dry soil between spreading roots (Fig. 7*b*). In any event, the watering of newly planted climbers is essential until they have become well established.

Honeysuckle

Even honeysuckle, which seems to grow in dry harsh conditions in the wild, needs careful tending until well established. Of all the climbing plants these cottage garden favourites are the most versatile. *Lonicera periclymenum* is the woodbine of our hedges and woods, a vigorous climber with whorls of richly fragrant cream and red flowers. Early Dutch honeysuckle is a variety of this called *belgica*, sporting purple flowers, which in favoured localities will be scenting the air during early summer. Late Dutch honeysuckle is the variety *serotina*. Rarely flowering until late summer this continues well into the autumn. All three kinds are of similar habit and appearance. So if you have sufficient room, a combination of all three ensures colour and fragrance throughout the season.

The evergreen *L. henryi* is scentless but very useful for providing a permanent screen. A happy inhabitant of north facing aspects, this interesting species produces small terminal clusters of pinkish blossoms during mid-summer, followed by conspicuous black fruits. The Japanese honeysuckle, *L. japonica*, is more vigorous than any of the foregoing, growing as much as 7 m (23 ft) in a single season. With this kind of growth, regular pruning is essential to keep the plant within bounds. There are several varieties, including *flexuosa* in which the creamy-white flowers and vigorous young shoots are flushed with purple. The variety *halliana* has flowers of a similar hue, while *aureo-reticulata* rarely flowers but is grown for its handsome gold and green reticulated foliage. This is the least energetic variety and is often cut to the ground during a severe winter.

Ivy

Not a problem likely to be encountered with the ivies. Certainly not with those derived from our native *Hedera helix*. These are all very tough and are available in a wide diversity of leaf shapes and colours. All prosper in cool conditions and are ideal for clothing north or east-facing walls. Contrary to popular belief, if the wall is in sound structural order, then the ivy is most unlikely to cause any problems. The brightest coloured one is 'Goldheart', a dark green leaf background splashed liberally with golden-yellow and showing a reddish cast in new shoots and juvenile foliage. An outstanding garden plant, but in need of careful placing in the cottage garden as it is so brightly coloured. Nevertheless it is probably the best of the ivy cultivars for colourfully cladding a wall in a relatively short space of time. Arrow-shaped leaves are provided by 'Sagittaefolia', crested ones by 'Cristata', while 'Marmorata' has foliage suffused with creamy-white and grey, producing a fine marbled finish.

The plain green-leaved ivies are equally attractive and I would encourage their use in many situations in the cottage garden rather than some of the more brash and outlandish kinds. The common Irish ivy, *H. hibernica*, differing very little in general aspect from our common *H. helix*, and the Himalayan ivy *H. nepalensis* which, in its adult non-clinging form, yields red or yellow decorative fruits. It is interesting to note that all ivies have three stages of growth, starting off as non-clinging scrambling plants which with age begin to ascend

Plants of all kinds throng the border, tying the house to the garden. The climbing rose softens harsh edges.

and cling by means of tiny suction roots to any nearby wall or substantial tree. Once established bushy adult foliage is produced which eventually yields relatively inconspicuous greenish-white flowers in crowded heads. These are followed by fruits of varying colours. If material is propagated from this arboreal growth, then so called tree ivies or arborescent ivies will be produced. These have all the characteristics of the adult ivy, but yield a neat rounded bush.

Ivies are traditionally climbers for northerly and easterly aspects, but it is not their prerogative alone, for the climbing hydrangea, *Hydrangea petiolaris*, also enjoys these conditions. A vigorous fellow capable of attaining enormous dimensions in its natural habitat, it is ideal for covering a wall. Entirely self-supporting, it produces bold white flowers amongst bright green foliage and although rather slow to start flowering is well worth waiting for. The same can be said of the wisteria, for this spectacular climber of the pea family needs several years before becoming properly established. Once flowering well it continues without faltering, producing richly scented chains of lilac-purple blossoms from late spring until midsummer. The usual kind is *Wisteria sinensis* which is available in a white form too, but there is also *W. floribunda* and this has yielded lavender and rose coloured forms of merit. To the casual observer both species look the same, but the flowers of *W. floribunda* open from the base of the raceme downwards, while in *W. sinensis* they open simultaneously.

Virginia creeper, Russian vine

It is not easy to sort out the various Virginia creepers, although this is of little account as all the species produce marvellous autumn colour. The most popular is *Parthenocissus tricuspidata*, for it is without doubt the purveyor of the most spectacular autumn tints. *Parthenocissus quinquefolia* is the true creeper from Virginia. This has distinctive five-lobed leaves rather like the bold irregular foliage of its name-sake.

Unlike that species, *P. quinquefolia* is not suited to a wall owing to its vigour. This is best exploited by allowing it to invade a mature tree turning it into a cascade of fiery red in the autumn.

The Russian vine, *Polygonum baldschuanicum* is another good climber for a tree. A vigorous twining vine-like plant, this has bright green, oval or heart-shaped leaves and panicles of tiny white flowers from mid to late summer. It requires a deep moist soil before giving of its best, but careful soil preparation will be well rewarded by the magnificent spectacle that it provides.

Passion flower

The passion flower, *Passiflora caerulea*, can be equally exciting, and while in general terms perhaps thought of as being an exotic, the best plants that I have ever seen have been on sunny walls in cottage gardens. Some gardeners dismiss the passion flower as tender, but the particular species under consideration is hardy in the greater part of the British Isles. The secret to its successful growth and flowering lies in the soil, for passiflora prefers a poor stony soil to encourage harsh growth, and yet not one so dry as to cause shrivelling of the young shoots. Rich soil encourages abundant growth at the expense of the flowers, growth which is so soft that it is easily damaged during the winter. Apart from the common blue-purple flowered species there is a reliable white cultivar called 'Constance Elliot'. Unlike the ordinary *Passiflora caerulea* which can be raised either from seed or cuttings, it is only cuttings that reproduce the true plant of 'Constance Elliot'.

The trumpet vine, *Campsis radicans*, is a similar proposition. Once established it makes an excellent cottage garden plant, and while benefitting from a southerly or westerly aspect, generally seems able to cope with the same kind of conditions under which clematis will grow. The best plant of this kind that I have ever seen clothes the east facing wall of an old cottage in East Anglia.

Right: For the larger garden scrambling shrub roses provide summer blossoms and autumn fruits.

Below: Climbing plants need not be grown in isolation: clematis and roses associate happily with one another.

The rose

However, the most usual climber for the cottage wall is the rose. Even non-gardeners yearn for roses around the door. None of the roses are true climbers in that they are self-supporting, but we must obviously include them here. All need tying in and training if they are to remain orderly. So the roses around the door have to be grown on a wooden framework, although this is quickly disguised once the plants become established. Selecting a climber or rambler can be fraught with difficulties if you wish to retain a cottage garden atmosphere, for many of the large flowered modern kinds are totally out of keeping. I have a strong affection for the old climbing 'Cecile Brunner', or sweetheart rose. This has tiny pink flowers with scarcely any scent borne in large clusters during early summer. It is a vigorous character which is just as at home in an old apple tree as around the front door. The rambler 'Albertine' is another good sort with coppery-pink flowers that smell of fresh fruit. Like the climbing 'Cecile Brunner' it is rather vigorous and can also be profitably accommodated in a small tree.

The diversity of roses available makes the choice very difficult. I love the old rambler 'Dorothy Perkins', even if it does suffer from mildew. This has vast clusters of small double pink flowers and rapidly growing, soft green foliage. My grandmother used this variety to disguise the outside privy, and a jolly good job it made too. Mildew disfigures it regularly unless you start spraying early, but with chemicals as good as benomyl available this is a minor inconvenience. 'Sander's White' is another rambler of similar habit, but fairly resistant to mildew. Amongst the climbers the soft pink 'New Dawn' is probably the pick of the cottage door roses, closely followed by a modern kind, the pink and apricot 'Compassion'. The bronzy-yellow 'Maigold' is often suggested as a golden flowered climber, but I would go for the plain unspoilt beauty of the single yellow 'Mermaid'.

5

HARDY ANNUALS AND BIENNIALS

Annual and biennial flowers have long been an integral part of the cottage garden scene. Of limited duration, these colourful plants are ideal for creating a quick effect on a new or raw site. They are equally useful for filling gaps in the mixed or herbaceous border and while no cottage garden would be complete without them, it should be appreciated that they are very labour intensive.

HARDY ANNUALS

Hardy annuals are of a single season's duration. That is, they are sown during the spring, they flower during the summer, and by the autumn they have expired. Being hardy it is usually possible to sow them directly in the open ground in the position in which you would like them to flower, thinning the seedlings as appropriate (Fig. 8). More detailed information is provided in the final chapter where I discuss the different methods of raising all cottage garden plants. For now I want to take an excursion through the seedsman's catalogue and extract as far as possible the plants and varieties that are appropriate to our project. Where better to start than amongst the marigolds.

Marigolds and mallow

The marigolds of the cottage garden are not the marigolds of the bedding plant trade. The bold characters of even stature with strange smelling leaves and garish blossoms that appear in every nursery, garden centre and greengrocers shop in the land at the beginning of summer are all members of the tagetes family. The marigold of the cottage garden and folk songs is the pot marigold or calendula. In fact the true English or pot marigold is *Calendula officinalis*. While this species is rarely grown on its own account now, there are many suitable cultivars around that can provide the same visual effect as the species, without the old mildew problems. Selection of cultivars needs to be careful though, for some of those derived from Japanese forms are so even and unreal as to be totally out of context with the informal comfortable atmosphere that we desire. Therefore modern cultivars like the uniform bright orange 'Geisha Girl' and soft yellow 'Lemon Queen' must be thoughtfully placed, although good mixtures such as the modern 'Family Circle' are easy to accommodate. Given an open sunny situation these colourful annuals will flourish, tolerating soil that is dry or damp, acid or alkaline with equal indifference.

I think that they are possibly the best colonizers of builders' rubbish that there are. If faced with uncompromising clay sub-soil, then make pot marigolds a priority. They are large seeded, easily handled, and can be sown in their final positions quite readily. Their only disadvantage is that unless great care is taken over the removal of fading blossoms, large quantities of viable seed will be scattered and you will be troubled with young plants for the foreseeable future. In the informality of a mixed border this can usually be tolerated, unless the progeny are from the seed produced by an F_1 hybrid. In this case it will almost certainly be very poor. Another reason to select older open pollinated strains of marigolds rather than brash modern hybrids.

Modern cultivars of the mallow, *Lavatera trimestris*, need treating with a similar reserve. They are perfectly acceptable if the

47

old plants are to be cleared and volunteer seeding is not to be allowed. Where cottage garden traditions are more strictly adhered to and chance seedlings are allowed to prosper, then it is important that from the outset only open pollinated non-F_1 hybrids are grown. These reproduce themselves more or less to type and, while without selection will tend to slowly deteriorate, produce quite tolerable plants even if allowed to regenerate for eight or ten years. All the mallows have bold mounds of glossy green leaves and spires of open cup or saucer-shaped blossoms. The species itself is pink and, although occasionally grown, was long since superseded by that old cottage garden favourite 'Loveliness'. In general garden terms the Fleuroselect award winning varieties 'Silver Cup' and 'Mount Blanc', which are pink and white flowered respectively, recently ousted 'Loveliness' from many seed catalogues. It is still available though, and I believe should be the mallow of our cottage garden. The seed of mallows is quite large and can be sown where the plants are intended to flower. If you have an excess of seedlings, then these are one of the few hardy annual types that will respond to transplanting.

Larkspur and cornflower

One of the others that can be dealt with in the same way if necessary is the larkspur. Not that the larkspur is a single entity, for there are at least two popular kinds derived from different annual species of delphinium. The rocket larkspur is the one that is usually associated with cottage gardening and is derived from *Delphinium ajacis*. It is skinny with feathery green foliage and tall lean spires of blossom in colours that vary from straightforward blue through mauve and pink to white. Several have been given names and are available individually. The other larkspur is of more recent popularity, and in decorative terms is far superior. Known as the imperial larkspur, modern strains have been derived directly from *D. consolida*. Typical of the perennial delphin-

Fig 8. Seed sowing in the open.

(*a*) Shuffle across the bed to firm the soil prior to sowing.

(*b*) Prepare a tilth with a rake.

(*c*) Mark out the site of each variety with a sprinkling of sand.

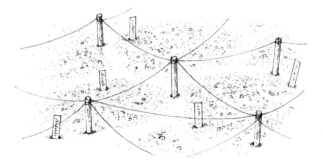

(*d*) Use pegs and black cotton to deter birds.

48

Limnanthes douglasii is a popular annual, affectionately referred to as the poached egg plant. A colourful subject for a sunny border.

ium, these have more substantial spikes of flowers that are excellent for cutting.

Larkspurs prefer an open, sunny situation, but because of their stature benefit from a little shelter from the wind and should in any event be provided with some twiggy support material while the plants are quite young. It is perfectly adequate to sow larkspurs during early spring in order to procure a summer display, but until recent times it was fashionable in the milder parts of the country to sow larkspur during early autumn for an early show.

The same was done with the cornflower, *Centaurea cyanus*, especially when early flowers were required for cutting. Like larkspur, the cornflower is a very hardy and amenable character well able to flourish in all but the driest and shadiest of situations. I really like the traditional blue cornflower, but have to admit that some of the mixed strains like 'Polka Dot' are really quite charming and would not in any way offend a cottage garden. All have stiff flower stems crowned with colourful ruffs of petals, and tough bluish-green foliage with a mealy bloom. This is absent from the slightly different, but closely related sweet sultan, *C. moschatus*, in which the foliage is brighter green and more refined. Its flower heads are equally distinctive, appearing quite fluffy and embracing a colour range that extends beyond the blues, whites and pinks of the cornflower to embrace yellow and deep wine as well. Only mixed strains are available from seedsmen, but these are first class, producing long lasting flowers on good strong stems.

Love-in-a-mist

Love-in-a-mist or devil-in-a-bush, *Nigella damascena*, is very good for cutting and an old cottage garden stalwart. It has bold soft blue flower heads surrounded by much divided wispy green foliage. 'Miss Jekyll' is the most popular blue cultivar and there is also a mixed strain called 'Persian Jewels' which is quite acceptable. Love-in-a-mist tolerates a wide range of conditions, but is better in the open where the soil is moist. Dryness at the roots causes stunted growth and poor flowering. If you garden on a heavy clay soil, then this is the plant for you. Once established it seeds itself freely and is all but in name a perennial, a habit shared by the poached egg plant, *Limnanthes douglasii*. The common name of this dwarf, sun-loving annual describes it well, the little daisy-like flowers being circular, with an inner portion of bright yellow and the outer edge creamy-white. A fragrant plant, it is useful for carpeting the ground in hot sunny spots where informality is the keynote.

Short growing hardy annuals

There are a number of short growing hardy annuals that are invaluable in the mixed border. Old friends like the Virginian stock; a cheery little fellow that will prosper in full sun with the minimum of attention. It flowers profusely with myriad tiny pinkish or purplish blossoms and seeds itself freely if left alone. It is not unlike the night-scented stock in many respects, although the latter will attain a height of 30 cm (1 ft) under favourable conditions. This is essentially an evening plant as its name suggests. It is not until the sun starts to sink that the blossoms begin to open, filling the air with a rich spicy fragrance. I consider night-scented stocks to be plants for growing beneath the living room window, where on a warm summer evening with the windows wide open their fragrance can be enjoyed to the full. In modern gardens they are patio plants, being raised nearer to the olfactory senses in tubs or planters. In the cottage garden this cannot be permitted, for patios and planters are clearly phenomena of our time and completely alien to the cottage garden.

Not so the candytuft, brightly coloured edging of the traditional annual border and a first class inhabitant of the informal flower garden. Modern plant breeding has developed a lot of bright and exciting new colours into candytuft; witness the vivid scarlet 'Red Flash'. Brave and beautiful

Ladies mantle, *Alchemilla mollis* provides a soft green foil for the blue
spires of delphiniums and frothy pink roses.

51

though these are and great for the modern suburban garden, they rest ill at ease amongst the subtle pastel shades of traditional cottage garden flowers. The old mixed strains still offered by some of the major seed companies are to be preferred as they have a charm and subtlety of colour unequalled by any of the hybridists recent progeny.

Clarkia and cosmos

There have been few new developments with the popular annual clarkia, even though there are some excellent named varieties around that have not been widely popularized. I think that the common mixture of clarkia grown by most gardeners is perfectly adequate. In our kind of garden it might be profitable to grow a few each of the old cultivars like the vivid scarlet 'Vesuvius' or snow-white 'Albatross' merely because it is often easier to place straight colour in the garden rather than mixtures. Also I believe that the cottage gardener should help to perpetuate plants that are part of his heritage and clearly these old cultivars fall into this category. So if you come across named clarkia varieties in a seed catalogue have a go and ensure their future.

If you have difficulty in obtaining any other than the mixed kind then not to worry, for these colourful mixtures are capable of satisfying the most discerning gardener. All have brightly coloured flowers on slender reddish stems which produce the most elegant soft green leaves. A native of California, clarkia enjoys a well-drained position in full sun, conditions also preferred by that other southern native, the common cosmos.

Widely distributed throughout Mexico, and the parent of most of the cosmos which we grow today, *Cosmos bipinnatus* is still sometimes found in its original form in old cottage gardens. A large feathery plant with striking saucer-shaped blossoms of lilac-purple, it is this that evokes for me the memories of old cottage gardens. However, if not over-planted, strains like 'Sensation'

in which the colour range extends from pale pink through lilac to red fit the bill adequately. Modern varieties like the recently introduced 'Diabolo' have a better habit than the species or the older cultivars, but lack much of the ungainly charm that they exhibit and produce flowers of hues that would have been unthinkable a mere half century ago. Some gardeners treat cosmos a bit like a bedding plant and start it under glass in seed trays. I have never found this necessary and when attempting to move young seedlings have often discovered that they do not re-establish very quickly; better to sow *in situ* in reasonably small drifts.

SPRING BEDDING BIENNIALS

It might be considered a fallacy to refer to all biennials as spring bedding, but in a cottage garden they usually are. Some are strictly perennials used as biennials, being sown during one summer, grown on until autumn, over-wintered and then encouraged into flower. Most of the plants coming under this heading are raised in the open ground and transplanted to their permanent positions during the autumn, although a few may be planted from boxes either in the autumn or in early spring while in bud. These latter comprise plants such as pansy, viola and polyanthus.

Wallflowers and forget-me-nots

Wallflowers and other spring flowering subjects which are associated with cottage gardens are often also important formal bedding subjects. As intimated earlier, formal bedding schemes are definitely out, so regard these plants in a different way and treat them as our great grandparents did; merely as additional plants for the border. As long as you choose the standard wallflower cultivars and avoid the true dwarfs, then this mental transition is not difficult to make. Use mixed strains like 'Fair Lady' or 'Persian Carpet' for making bold drifts of

Lupins of the Russell Strain stand to attention in this colourful
herbaceous border.

colour, but utilize single colours such as 'Blood Red' and 'Cloth of Gold,' for filling gaps in mixed plantings.

Wallflowers are the gilliflowers of old, not only providing rich colour for the late spring garden, but filling the air with a sweet fragrance. If they remain in good health following flowering allow them to remain, for strictly perennials, they will develop a woody framework and take on the venerable look that wallflowers in cottage gardens should have. Do not forget that other wallflower *Cheiranthus allionii*, which the botanists now tell us is not a wallflower at all, but which will remain with me as the Siberian wallflower for ever. I have mentioned elsewhere how useful this bright orange, sweetly scented perennial plant can be when associated with the lovely white *Iris florentina*. However, that is not its only great association for it can be mixed with the azure hummocks of forget-me-not with tremendous effect.

Forget-me-nots are great traditional plants of the cottage garden, but ones which deteriorate quickly if not properly maintained. Always grow fresh plants each year if you wish to maintain quality as most cultivars are truly biennial. If they seem to persist it is unlikely that the same plants are flowering each year. Usually it is seed that has dropped into the centre of the crown that germinates and produces what appears to be a perennial plant that the gardener believes is 'reverting'. Individual forget-me-not plants do not revert, but strains deteriorate with each succeeding generation if not rigorously reselected and nowadays a number of the cultivars popularly grown are of F_1 origin.

The only forget-me-not that is truly perennial and likely to find a place in the cottage garden is the moisture-loving *Myosotis scorpioides*. Sometimes its selected form 'Semperflorens' is grown as a perennial in the mixed border on heavy soil or where there is a damp or waterlogged patch. Otherwise the named kinds should be replaced each year after flowering. At present there is little to choose in popularity between 'Blue Ball' and 'Royal Blue', and if you need a white form there is a variety referred to as *alba* offered by one or two seedsmen. Myosotis are best produced as boxed plants for transplanting during the autumn. Open ground plants are very difficult to manage and almost impossible to get established unless you remove them to their permanent quarters very early in their life. Apart from their value as low growing plants for the front of the border, all the forget-me-nots mix well visually with old fashioned tulips of various kinds and offset the bright colours of wallflowers. Alone they are a little frothy and misty, but as a foil or contrast they are superb.

Polyanthus and pansies

You could not say the same about the polyanthus, for these are available in a wide range of brilliant colours which can be used to highlight particular garden features. They need using with an element of caution, for some of the more recent hybrids tend to have an iridescence that gives a certain brashness that is not in keeping with our concept. Some of the older, smaller flowered and cheaper strains are the most appropriate. Avoid any of the 'Pacific Giants', the blue-flowered hybrids and those derived from the 'Cowichan Strain'. Admirable though all of these are, none are really compatible with the spring garden as I see it. If you can get hold of a few of the old named varieties that can only be increased by division after flowering, then do so. These were the true inhabitants of the cottage garden, along with fairly mediocre seed raised plants. I am not suggesting that mediocrity be brought into the garden, but where a lot of plants are needed or economy is the order of the day, then select a popular mixture of a seed-house strain. Good colour forms can always be selected and divided to bulk up stocks of desirable plants.

Most pansies have now become so far removed from the little heartsease *Viola*

Left: Foliage as well as flowers provide a lasting contrast in this tastefully planted mixed border.

Below: Bold colours provide useful focal points, when subtly mixed with pastel shades.

tricolor, that it is difficult to include them in the cottage garden. I much prefer the faceless violas, for these are of smaller size and equal diversity with a flowering period that often outlasts its cousins. Most are derived from *V. cornuta*, a most useful blue-flowered plant itself which can be raised from cuttings as well as seed. There are separate colours available, but I much prefer a rustic-looking mixture like 'Toyland'. Seed raising is perfectly adequate for this, but do replace the plants each year and weed out any self-sown seedlings. Violas grown well are a great asset, when repeat flowering or growing as second generation accidents they are a disaster. If you must grow pansies, and on reflection perhaps you should, then do not be any more ambitious than trying 'Swiss Giants'. This strain has all the colours that you are likely to require in acceptable shades and the flowers are weatherproof and of sensible dimensions. A new cultivar that I have recently tried in which the flower size is modest and the varying colouration pleasing is called 'Duet'. Splendid little plants of similar stature to the bedding violas provided a scintillating show of restful colour from late spring until the first sharp autumn frost.

Other biennials

Another plant that gives value for money, but of which I am always rather nervous, is the double daisy, *Bellis perennis*, a form of our native wild daisy. Technically a perennial, this is another case where it should be treated as a biennial, for if left to seed, a host of undesirable weedy seedlings will become established not only in the border, but in the lawn as well. The majority of popular strains are in shades of pink, red and white and are derived from the full double form of the daisy called *monstrosum*. There are also a few separate named cultivars about like the red flowered 'Etna' and soft pink 'Alice'.

Named varieties are also making an appearance amongst the sweet williams, although none have acquired great popularity. Every gardener that I have spoken to regards the mixed auricula-eyed strains of sweet williams as unbeatable. I have to admit that, for vigour and reliability, I have to agree. Treated as wallflowers they can go on for ever. Well almost, for they are truly perennials and if looked after as such and regularly fed will come up with a good show for a few years.

Relatives of the pinks and therefore within the embrace of the dianthus, they revel in a well-drained, alkaline soil in full sun. I think that they are excellent as members of the mixed or herbaceous border, but many gardeners grow them for their top quality cut flowers. Whatever your justification, they are important members of the cottage garden, providing colour and character at that in-between time after the spring flush has finished but before summer blossoming has commenced. Apart from conventional sweet williams there are some annual ones available from certain nurseries that can be sown in early spring for flowering the same year.

6

TENDER AND BEDDING ANNUALS

This little group is not all it seems, for I have no intention of discussing formal bedding schemes as they find no place in the cottage garden. Nor are all the plants under examination truly annuals, for a number of so-called 'bedding' subjects are technically tender perennials that we just treat as annuals. Having cleared up all these apparent anomalies we should look at what is intended. For my part I feel that the plants which rightly belong here are some of the older cultivars of those which require initial greenhouse protection. They may well be subjects that under different circumstances would form the main part of a formal bedding design, but I hope that by viewing them slightly differently their usefulness in the mixed border will become apparent.

Asters and antirrhinums

I am thinking particularly now of the marvellous shaggy ostrich plume asters and their single counterparts the *sinensis* asters. These have for many years been inextricably bound up in the mixed cottage or country garden. Not just because they provide suitable form and colour, but because they are excellent for cutting too. There are a whole range of named cultivars and strains in all the major divisions of the aster kingdom, but be careful about your selection as many of the better ones have too formal an aspect. Also be aware of the confusion that can arise between the garden aster and the plant that is known botanically as *Aster*. The latter name truly belongs with the perennial plants which we affectionately call Michaelmas daisies. *Callistephus* is the name of the true garden asters, all of which are tender and of annual duration.

I always feel that it is prudent to provide the snap dragon, or antirrhinum with the same cultural conditions as the aster. Although very different plants, both have similar cultural problems. On the one hand the antirrhinum is almost hardy and when established virtually indestructible, but like the aster it can be very tricky in the early stages of growth. Both are very prone to damping off and neither seems to enjoy being raised in other than a soil-based compost. Indeed, asters that are raised on soilless compost and then planted out into a heavy loam or clay soil rarely prosper. Raising in the nearest material to that ultimately to be experienced is the easiest way of weaning asters to natural garden conditions. Antirrhinums are not so fussy once they are growing away strongly, but the initial problems of raising seedlings, especially if you do not have good greenhouse conditions can be considerable.

Notwithstanding these difficulties both parties are excellent for cottage gardens, although some of the brighter and taller antirrhinums will need careful placing, as well as the dwarf carpet bedding types like 'Sweetheart'. The only other rule to follow is the selection of a strain that is rust resistant. Most good antirrhinum varieties are now immune to this devasting and incurable affliction which is quite clearly recognizable by the descriptive common name. While writing in depressing tones, I perhaps ought to also mention aster wilt, an equally devastating and incurable disease for which there are no true wilt resistant cultivars. This causes the wilting and collapsing of plants that have just started to become established. If you have aster wilt in your garden just forget asters and grow something else.

Pinks, carnations and verbenas

What about some of the annual dianthus or pinks and carnations? Nowadays there are some superb strains about, many of which are made for cottage garden display. The modern Fleuroselect winning 'Telstar', a much refined and long-flowering sweet william-like pink with a colour range that embraces all the old fashioned shades. True carnation-type flowers can be provided by the dwarf 'Profusion' strain or 'Dwarf Fragrance' cultivars. If the stems were a bit longer they could be cut and you would think that they were florists' carnations. Taller strains of pinks and carnations are not really suited to the kind of garden that we envisage, they are really more for cutting than general display.

All the popular kinds are easily raised from seed sown under glass during early spring, although I have raised the dwarf Indian pink *Dianthus chinensis* and its variety *heddewigii* from seed sown in free-draining soil in the open during late spring and flowered them with great success. Given an alkaline soil and a bright sunny situation they are amongst the most reliable of annual flowers.

Indeed, I would say that they could only be equalled in reliability by the Victorian verbenas. Those lovely plants of a bygone era derived from the plant known as *Verbena venosa*, but now itself irreverently changed by botanists to *V. rigida*. I recall as a student taking cuttings of these lovely creatures in later summer for over-wintering in an unheated greenhouse, to be potted in the spring for the following season's bedding display. Truly the verbenas are perennials, but in days gone by it was not possible to raise plants, other than the true species, satisfactorily from seed. In recent years development work has continued apace so that now there are a number of very good straight colours as well as mixed strains. Most of these have been developed in the United States and are increasingly finding their way into our seed catalogues. I feel that few of the individual colours are as subdued as their Victorian forebears and therefore are perhaps dubious propositions for the cottage garden. However, a mixed strain like 'Showtime' should provide all that we seek.

If a good colour is spotted in a particular batch of plants there is no reason why we cannot revert to the old practice of taking cuttings if only a few plants are going to be required. Although the parentage of modern verbenas is somewhat more complicated than hitherto and botanists even deem the progeny as *V. hortensis*, I feel that they are essentials of the cottage garden.

Not so the petunias, salvias, nemesias and lobelias of the present day. These do not truly belong here, even though by careful integration with appropriate plants it is possible to make a pleasing overall picture. Nor really do the modern stocks, even though stocks of one kind or another have occurred in the literature of country gardens for centuries. Modern varieties of stock are extremely attractive and can be utilized without much effort. They are especially valuable as they are of similar appearance to their grandparents, but now we can ensure that every plant produces double flowers in selected races. Traditionally stocks have been grown for their scent and it was just hoped that most of the seedlings transplanted would be double and provide an added visual attraction.

Plant breeders have worked extensively on stocks during recent years and it is now possible to select double flowered plants at the seedling stage. To do this, seed should be sown during early spring in a temperature of 15°C (59°F). Once all the seedlings have germinated and their seed leaves have unfurled the temperature should be lowered to about 7°C (45°F) for two or three days. The seedlings will alter their colour, the single ones becoming darker and the double ones being pale green. It is the lighter coloured seedlings that are obviously desirable and the ones to be pricked out and grown on. Reselection is done at the four leaf stage and any seedlings that are developing

Lawns are a feature that give an illusion of space. A well-constructed path
is the lifeline of the garden.

weakly are also discarded as these are likely to be odd singles missed during the initial rogueing. It is vital for stocks to have an open sunny situation in a well drained soil. All recent varieties could be considered to be suitable for the cottage garden as the blossoms are still all in attractive pastel hues and the flower spikes well proportioned. The only caution that I would add is to your expectations from these traditional plants. That term 'ten weeks' when applied to a stock is very open to question. Very rarely can stocks raised from seed be seen in flower within ten weeks.

SWEET PEAS

Sweet peas epitomize the cottage garden flower. Not that the sweet peas which we grow today were anything like the original ones grown by the early cottagers of England. Although introduced by a Sicilian monk in the late 1690s, it was not until well into the 1800s that Henry Eckford first made any progress with them towards a reliable garden flower. Finally it was Silas Cole, head gardener to the Earl Spencer who made the major breakthrough that was to lead to the introduction of the present day Spencer sweet peas. Since then a number of different categories have arisen, embracing the multifloras galaxies and dwarfs. The cultivars that you select from these are a matter of personal choice. Sweet peas are available in a wide variety of colours and each season sees new introductions, most of which will be in keeping with our theme. It seems almost impossible to produce a brash or bilious sweet pea variety.

The Spencer sweet peas are tall growing plants, with frilled blossoms and a delicious fragrance, while the multifloras are less substantial but have an earlier flowering period. Galaxies have a large quantity of blossoms per stem but flower at the same time as the Spencers, while the dwarf kinds have typical sweet pea blossoms on much shorter plants.

Sowing and planting

Sweet peas can either be sown in the autumn and overwintered in a frame, or else started off under glass in the spring. A late spring sowing outside is also possible, although the flowering period is considerably shortened. Autumn sown sweet peas should always be grown in John Innes Seed Compost so that they do not make excessive soft growth before the onset of bad weather, whereas during early spring, when the compost takes a while to warm up, it is more prudent to use the lighter and warmer soilless type.

Irrespective of sowing season it is preferable to adopt the same cultural routine. Remember that sweet peas are members of the legume family and like other related plants dislike root disturbance. It is theoretically possible to transplant misplaced or additional seedlings successfully, but in practice they always suffer a check. That is why the majority of growers raise their plants in sweet pea tubes. These are made of a thick black papery material called whalehide with a narrow top, deep sides and no base. Filled with compost and stood pot thick in trays they are the best way that I know of raising vigorous young plants. If two seeds are sown in each pot, the stronger seedling can be allowed to remain. Although with some mixtures it is wise to take a cross section of plant stature as different colours have different vigours. If you select all the stronger seedlings from a mixed batch you always end up with a preponderance of blue or purplish colours.

The plants must be carefully hardened off before planting outside if they have been raised in a glasshouse; good soil is an equal partner in the production of quality sweet peas and adequate preparation and the incorporation of well-rotted manure the previous autumn is a prerequisite. This latter is especially important as bud and flower drop are common maladies associated with a variable soil moisture content. A high humus content in the soil encourages a consistent moisture level.

Pelargoniums are colourful and can be used in many situations. The
hollow log is an imaginative container.

61

Supporting sweet peas

At planting time it is vital to include your supports, as the pushing and poking with sticks or stakes around and amongst young plants after planting can be very damaging. There are several methods of supporting sweet peas, but the one that merits prime consideration in the informal garden involves the use of clumps of brush wood. These are made from very twiggy material, usually birch, and are pushed into the soil in a circle so that a twiggy column about 2 m (6½ ft) high is created. If such material is not forthcoming, then a similar effect can be obtained by making a strong columnar or pyramidal framework over which netting can be stretched. This need not be of the permanent wire sort, but of the plastic material used extensively in the vegetable garden. Of course sweet peas can also be allowed to grow in and amongst other plants, but I have found maintenance very trying, although in the short term the effect is good. Sweet peas for garden decoration are allowed to develop naturally without pinching or removing tendrils. Such extravagances are for the showman, but having said that, if a sweet pea has not naturally broken and started to produce laterals by the time that it is 15 cm (6 in) high it should be pinched out. Otherwise routine summer maintenance merely involves watering regularly in spells of dry weather and removing faded blossoms and their stalks regularly to encourage a longer flowering season.

7
HARDY HERBACEOUS PERENNIALS

Hardy herbaceous perennials is a very loose term that covers a multitude of plants. Correctly it refers to plants of many years' duration which die right down to the ground each winter. In reality they are often deemed to be plants with shorter life spans which self-perpetuate from seed, or some of the woody sub-shrubs which rarely disappear completely during the winter. In cottage gardens herbaceous perennials have always been grown in borders, and even though the modern trend towards island beds makes sense in the modern small garden, it is totally out of keeping with the traditions of cottage gardening.

An island bed is one to which the observer has unhindred access, larger plants being grown in the centre and shorter ones towards the edge. Not only does this present a better view of the plants, but enables them to support one another in a natural manner. A traditional herbaceous border, or a mixed border in which herbaceous and shrubby plants co-exist has a background of a wall, fence or hedge and the plants are arranged so that taller subjects occupy the rear area, gradually grading down so that the shorter plants are at the front. In the cottage garden the herbaceous border has had a strong tradition, but smaller gardens today usually have to compromise and both shrubs and annuals share the same area.

PREPARATION AND PLANTING

Soil preparation
Good soil preparation is essential with herbaceous borders, and for areas to be devoted in mixed borders to hardy perennial plants,

as it is likely to be several years before the plants are lifted and divided. Therefore the opportunity should be taken to incorporate as much organic matter into the soil as possible during the preparation. Well-rotted garden compost, strawy manure and leaf mould are all excellent soil conditioners and help maintain moisture without waterlogging. Perennial weeds should be eliminated from any area to be given over to herbaceous plants. Couch grass, creeping thistle and other common pernicious weeds can cause endless trouble once established amongst border plants. Their creeping rootstocks become entangled in the fibrous roots of the desirable plant and create a reservoir of problems for the future. Only when established herbaceous plants are lifted and divided can these be removed successfully.

Handpicking of perennial weeds is useful, but more certain results can be obtained by using a weedkiller containing glyphosate. This is a translocated weedkiller which is absorbed by the foliage of the weed and then transmitted throughout the sap stream, killing the plant entirely but not polluting the soil. Early spring is the ideal time to make an application, just as the plants are beginning to shoot, for the chemical is more readily absorbed and translocated at this time. Spraying in spring usually catches any pieces of root missed during handpicking as these will also be producing small shoots.

There is not a lot of difference between planting a new border and refurbishing an existing one. An existing border will doubtless contain a number of plants that resent disturbance, or in the mixed border there will doubtless be shrubs that must be worked around. Some herbaceous subjects resent disturbance so much that they sulk and refuse to flower for several years after being moved – plants like paeony and Christmas rose as well as any members of the pea family, such as Russell lupins. These must all remain where they are, unless they are exhausted, when plants like lupins can be increased by cuttings of young shoots taken as they emerge from the crown in early spring.

Once soil preparation is completed, the areas which various groups of plants are going to occupy can be marked out with sand. It is useful to have an idea of where you are going to put each plant variety and I find a rough sketch on paper a useful guide. Do not be hide-bound by your original ideas as these were in all probability made at the kitchen table and imagination and reality do not always tie up. Use the sketch as a basis upon which to work. Do not be so dogmatic that you have no flexibility. As long as certain basic principles are adhered to there is little that can go wrong in the planning of a mixed or herbaceous border. The arrangement of colour and contrast is purely personal, so are shapes and heights, and their combinations. What is not flexible is the quantity of plants necessary to create a satisfactory effect. Single plants do not create an attractive picture, nor in a cottage garden context do square, circular or oblong blocks of plants. Do what you wish about colours and contrasts, but stick to groups of five, seven or nine plants and arrange them in an irregular fashion.

Planting

Herbaceous plants can be planted at any period during the dormant season. This lasts from mid-autumn until early spring, although it is possible now to plant container grown perennials all the year round. Unfortunately this restricts the diversity of plant material at your disposal as only plants that do well in containers are sold that way. It is also likely to be hot and dry during the summer and container grown plants need constant nursing in order that they become established, watering being of the utmost

importance. If you have to plant during the summer months from containers, then ensure that the potball of each plant is thoroughly soaked before planting. If the plant has been in its container for a long period of time the rootstock may have become very woody and may well need teasing out before planting. Roots that are growing in a congested corkscrew fashion and which become hard and woody rarely break out of their rootball and ramify the surrounding soil without assistance.

Traditional autumn or spring planting presents none of these difficulties. All that is required is that each plant is firmly planted in a hole which is of sufficient dimensions to ensure that the fibrous roots are not cramped or congested. Some herbaceous plants become totally dormant during the winter and do not even leave a reminder of their presence in the form of a woody withered flower stalk. These all require marking with a small cane after planting. The soil all looks the same once the plants are in as it is very difficult to remember what was planted where. Liberal applications of slug pellets amongst the most vulnerable plants like lupins and delphiniums is a necessary precaution, for plants like this produce succulent shoots during early spring which are the delight of these slimy predators. A ring of weathered soot or ash around each group of vulnerable plants is a good slug deterrent.

Freshly acquired plants are ready prepared for planting, but if you are reorganizing your own border you will obviously wish to retain some of each of your existing stock. Most will be capable of division, the easiest and most reliable means of increasing them and ensuring that they remain true to type. Some border plants produce single vigorous tap roots and are indivisible. These are the ones that are usually reproduced from seed or short stem cuttings. Plants with an abundant growth of fibrous root are the ones most suited to division. Established clumps of perennials should be carefully lifted with a garden fork and as much of the surplus soil as possible shaken off the roots.

Moisture loving perennials throng this streamside. Many plants that will not tolerate ordinary border conditions can be grown here.

The earlier that this can be done during the autumn the easier the task will be, especially if you garden on heavy soil. To separate the clumps, insert two garden forks back to back and lever one against the other (Fig. 9).

Fig 9. Dividing perennials. Insert two forks back to back and lever apart.

Individual offsets can then be selected for replanting. Any woody material in the centre of the clump should be discarded, even if it looks strong and vigorous, it is the young healthy shoots from around the edge that are likely to produce the best plants.

SOME SHADY CHARACTERS

Gardeners invariably consider shady beds and borders to be a liability. Places in which to plant periwinkle and rose of sharon or maybe a fern or two. This is regrettable, for there are a whole host of shade-loving subjects which can turn a dark corner into one of the most interesting parts of the garden. Of these the hellebores are amongst the most useful, for not only do they cope well with difficult shady conditions, but brighten up the garden in the dark and dreary days of winter. With their attractive, waxen blossoms they stand defiant against weather that has swept their summer flowering contemporaries away.

Christmas and Lenten roses

The Christmas rose, *Helleborus niger*, is the first to flower, with blooms occasionally appearing during late autumn. These are held aloft on stout erect stems, glistening white saucers with central clusters of rich lemon stamens. If protected from rain splashes with a sheet of glass raised on a few bricks, they will be excellent for cutting. *Helleborus atrorubens* flowers at the same time of the year with tightly bunched heads of plum coloured blossoms. Although reluctant to bloom until well established, once settled down it does so profusely, casting viable seed in all directions and rapidly forming a vigorous colony of young plants. So will *H. corsicus*, now more correctly called *H. argutifolius*. By no means as flamboyant, its huge heads of soft apple-green blossoms have a quaint and endearing charm which has captured the hearts of the flower-arranging fraternity. Being produced continuously from late winter until spring, they are excellent value, their cane-like stems and spiny glaucous foliage adding a further dimension.

The Lenten rose *H. orientalis* is very much a cottage garden plant, but flowers rather later during mid and late spring. It is of the same general aspect as the Christmas rose, but with flowers that vary in colour from pale cream to deep plum and are variously spotted and flecked with purple or black. All the hellebores are easily grown in a shady spot if left undisturbed. They appreciate a soil with plenty of organic matter incorporated into it, and benefit from an annual mulch of peat or well-rotted manure immediately after flowering.

Hostas and lily of the valley
Hostas or plantain lilies enjoy similar treatment. These are some of the most reliable and decorative foliage plants for the garden and were very popular during the hey-day of the cottage garden. A lull in popularity followed between the wars, but once again they have come to the fore especially in the gardens of those who indulge in floral art. Their names are in a dreadful muddle, so it is best to go to a nursery or garden centre during late spring when their leaves have just unfurled and select them by sight. The majority of gardeners agree that of the variegated leafed varieties the most desirable is *Hosta undulata medio-variegata*, a colourful fellow with slightly contorted foliage in vividly contrasting splashes of white, cream and green. The large leafed hybrid 'Thomas Hogg' has more orderly bright green leaves with a fairly uniform pure white margin, while the dubiously named *H. glauca marginata* is equally striking and a distinct variety of the best plain blue-green leaved species *H. glauca*.

I always regard *H. plantaginea*, with its big heart-shaped leaves and delicately fragrant white trumpet shaped blossoms as the aristocrat of the family. Better even than the ubiquitous *H. fortunei* and its forms. *Hosta lancifolia* is smaller than the others and has long stalked racemes of lavender-blue flowers. Several different forms are around, but I think that the golden-green foliage cultivar 'Aurea' is the best.

Foliage counts for little with that old cottage garden favourite the lily of the valley, *Convallaria majalis*, for this most popular of shade lovers is grown for its dainty pendant white blossoms and its indescribably delicious fragrance. It is a true woodland plant, preferring a cool moist root-run in a peaty soil. If provided with conditions to its liking it grows profusely, carpeting the soil with a sheet of tightly knit, glaucous foliage. Established colonies resent disturbance, but there comes a time when it is necessary to curb their exuberance, or perhaps you may wish to start a new group

somewhere else. This is best done during early autumn when the plants are dormant. Lift the tangled mass of roots and separate out the small white crowns or 'pips' and replant just beneath the soil surface. Apart from the popular white species, there is a fully double cultivar called 'Plena', the large flowered 'Fortin's Giant' and the pale violet-rose 'Rosea'.

Sweet violets and foxgloves
Sweet violets, *Viola odorata*, always associate well with lily of the valley, enjoying much the same kind of conditions. They have been grown by generations of cottagers, reaching the height of popularity during the late nineteenth century, but subsequently waning until now it is difficult to obtain any named kind other than the old faithful 'Governor Herricks'. If you come across 'Princess of Wales' or 'Swanley White' then snap them up, for they are the best of the old fashioned cut flower varieties. Young plants should be planted out in well-prepared soil during late spring, spacing them about 20 cm (8 in) apart. Keep well watered until established and ensure that they are weed-free as they are susceptible to a disease called crown rot if air cannot circulate freely. During autumn it is useful to give a surface dressing of wood ash as this acts as a soil conditioner and slug deterrent. Flowering takes place from autumn until spring depending upon variety. If you do as I like to do and utilize them as cut flowers, then take a leaf out of grandmother's book and cut the blossoms in the early morning with the dew still on them. Immerse the cut stems in a bucket of cold water for a couple of hours. This ensures prolonged vase life.

Foxgloves are not flowers for cutting, but most useful for hostile, shaded conditions. Most gardeners know our native foxglove, *Digitalis purpurea*, not only a common plant of country gardens, but of woodlands and hedgerows on acid soil throughout Britain. In its natural form it is a tall, erect and rather coarse biennial or perennial with grey-green leaves and long terminal racemes of tubular rosy-purple or white flowers. A rather bizarre variety known as *campanulata* has large bell-shaped terminal blossoms, while a race known as *gloxinaeflora* produces multi-coloured blossoms liberally splashed and spotted with maroon.

Apart from *D. purpurea* only one other biennial species is commonly encountered and that is the appropriately named *D. ferruginea*. A native of southern Europe, but equally at home in the cottage garden, this tall and stately fellow produces handsome well-formed spikes of hairy, rust-red flowers above large smooth green leaves. A complete contrast to the charming crushed strawberry hued *D. mertonensis*. Allegedly a perennial, I have never succeeded in keeping this for any longer than a couple of seasons, possibly owing to the hairy nature of its stems and foliage and the not inconsiderable dampness of my garden.

Digitalis lutea, however, thrives and seeds itself freely. Although the least distinctive of the foxglove species, with its small glabrous leaves and tubular canary-yellow flowers in long dense racemes, it does flower for much of the summer in dry dusty conditions which suit few other plants.

Solomon's seal and butchers' broom

One of the exceptions though, is Solomon's seal, *Polygonatum multiflorum*, a well known and widely cultivated, old-fashioned plant with a thick creeping rhizome from which arise arching stems of fresh glaucous leaves and legions of pendent, greenish-white blossoms. A smaller version, *P. multiflorum nanum* grows scarcely 30 cm (1 ft) high and has tiny tubular white blossoms, while *P. roseum* sports flowers of a soft pinkish hue. The closely allied *Smilacina racemosa*, although having no strong cottage garden traditions, fits in rather well in the general scene. Of similar habit to the Solomon's seal, smilacina is rather more startling with its bold, plumrose panicles of creamy-white blossoms followed by bright red berries. An excellent plant for dry, shady conditions.

Dry shade also provides a home for the sub-shrubby butchers, broom, *Ruscus aculeatus*, a prickly evergreen plant. There are both male and female kinds, the latter producing shiny red fruits when there is a male in the vicinity. There is a slightly dwarfer hermaphrodite form about which I know little and which is rather dubiously sold by nurserymen as *R. aculeatus hermaphroditus*. This should not be confused with the creeping *R. hypoglossum*, for this has each sex on a separate plant. Together with the somewhat doubtfully distinct *R. hypophyllum*, *R. hypoglossum* produces larger, almost leaf-like cladodes and is excellent for carpeting hostile ground beneath mature trees.

HARDY FERNS AND ORNAMENTAL GRASSES

Hardy ferns

The hardy ferns were very much a part of the cottage garden. Unfortunately many of the extremely fine named kinds grown during Victorian times were irretrievably lost during the First World War and their popularity subsequently waned. They are now seeing a marked revival and despite the lack of improved garden varieties, there are still enough species, forms and old selections in cultivation to satisfy the most discerning gardener.

Our native male fern, *Dryopteris filix-mas*, is undoubtedly one of the most useful, for it will thrive in almost any soil or situation. A coarse growing plant of dignified stature with broad lance-shaped fronds, it attains a height of a metre (yard) or more. Its opposite number the lady fern, *Athyrium filix-femina*, is equally tolerant of situation, but a trifle more elegant in structure. With graceful arching fronds it has been the delight of gardeners for many years and under the influence of cultivation has given rise to many very attractive forms and varieties. Both the hard shield fern, *Polystichum aculeatum*, and soft shield fern, *P. setiferum*,

Left: Amongst this galaxy of spring flowering plants are our native Pasque flower, *Pulsatilla vulgaris* and the common rock cress, *Arabis alpina.*

Below: Delphiniums give colour to the garden in early summer. They are easily raised from seed and flower the following year.

sport bright green scaly fronds that remain in character until well after Christmas. The closely related holly fern, *P. lonchitis* is completely evergreen and with the hard fern, *Blechnum spicant*, lends height and colour to the garden during the winter months.

For poolside planting few ferns can surpass the tall and stately royal fern, *Osmunda regalis*, its handsome fronds being mirrored in the water as they change colour from lime-green through yellow to bronze. Unfortunately these delightful autumnal tints are short-lived, for at the first touch of frost the leaflets shrivel and hang wearily from the semi-persistent frond stalks. Often grown in association with the royal fern, the sensitive fern, *Onoclea sensibilis* thrives where its spreading rhizomes are allowed to creep into the water and colonize the shallower areas. Its fronds are flattened, about 30 cm (1 ft) high and change from rose-pink to an agreeable shade of pale green as the summer progresses. The ostrich fern, *Matteucia struthiopteris*, appreciates a similar position, thrusting up handsome pea-green fronds like huge lacy shuttlecocks. Under favourable conditions these may reach a metre in height and produce curious dense spikes of rusty coloured spores from the centre of each plant.

In drier shady places the hart's tonge fern, *Asplenium scolopendrium*, and its various crested and crimped varieties may be tried. This is a tough little fellow with broad solid fronds some 45 cm (18 in) long that resemble dock leaves rather than fronds. They are more or less evergreen, persisting until early spring when the young emerging fronds take over. The small divided fronds of the common polypody, *Polypodium vulgare* are almost evergreen too, but this little fern requires much damper conditions. In nature it grows amongst moss on old walls and boulders and consequently prefers these conditions in garden situations.

The various spleenworts inhabit similar places and are excellent subjects for the rock garden. This is a rather doubtful feature in the cottage garden, but crevices in old walls serve equally well if one is being a purist and excluding alpine gardening altogether. Certainly spleenworts, like the tiny maidenhair spleenwort, *Asplenium trichomanes* and the black spleenwort, *A. adiantum-nigrum*, would have been utilized by the cottage gardener and can still be seen in such gardens to this day, especially in the damper regions of Britain. The maidenhair spleenwort has slender arching fronds which support legions of tiny round leaflets for their entire length, while its cousin the black spleenwort has attractive triangular fronds on slender black stalks.

Ornamental grasses

Decorative grasses are very much underrated in the ornamental garden, yet they provide such a diversity of shape size and colour. Almost all fit in well with a cottage garden atmosphere even if they are not strictly of the correct historical period. The only grasses that I have doubts about using in situations that we are envisaging are the bamboos and pampas grass, despite the fact that one or two of the former were popularly grown, for the production of canes.

The annual grasses are amongst the most useful in the cottage garden, not only for decoration, but for cutting and drying for floral art work. Some are hardy and can be sown in the open ground from early spring onwards although in northern areas early summer is probably a more satisfactory time. Except for decorative maize, which is best raised in individual pots like sweet corn, all the other popular annual kinds can be sown where they are to flower, crowded seedlings being thinned during the summer as necessary.

I love the delicate little quaking grass, *Briza maxima*, with its tiny yellowish lantern-like seeds, and the decorative barley, *Hordeum jubatum*. The foxtail millet, *Setaria italica*, is another striking annual grass beloved of the flower arranger. It is a loose tufted plant, up to 90 cm (3 ft) high with heavy, bristly, green flower spikes and

Lupins and iris are cottage garden favourites which are tolerant of most soils and situations, here seen dominating this narrow border.

handsome, bluish-green foliage. *Polypogon monospeliensis* has one of the trickiest Latin names, but is one of the easiest annual grasses to grow. Popularly called the annual beard grass, it produces lovely silky inflorescences amongst fresh green foliage.

The hare's tail grass *Lagurus ovatus*, also has silky flower heads, but they are much broader and produced on stout stems about 90 cm (3 ft) high. A good drying grass, in its dwarf cultivar 'Nana' it is an excellent front of border subject. Maize is a bit of a novelty, but does associate well with other cottage garden plants, especially if you choose the less brash squaw corn, *Zea mays*, and its varieties. All have decorative foliage and cobs in which the kernels are multicoloured.

Most perennial grasses are cottage garden favourites, but need careful watching if they are not to become invasive. Especially the common variegated gardener's garters, *Phalaris arundinacea* 'Picta'. It has a look-alike in *Glyceria aquatica* 'Variegata', which unlike phalaris is a water dweller. One of the easiest marginal subjects for the garden pool, it has boldly striped green and cream foliage which is deep rose-pink in early spring. *Elymus glaucus* provides another unique foliage colour. Sold by nurseries under this name, it is truly the lyme grass, *E. arenarius*. Nevertheless, the fact that it is a native does not mean that it is not garden worthy. Flourishing in hot, dry, hostile soil conditions it delights with its creeping sea of steely blue foliage. Its flowers are not very exciting and best removed when first seen in order to maintain a tidy appearance. *Festuca glauca* also has blue foliage, but in tight, impenetrable clumps. One of the easiest perennial grasses to raise from seed it is often used by gardeners as an annual.

The stipas are tall handsome characters that are also readily raised from seed. They are grasses for every garden, especially the graceful and free-flowering *Stipa calamagrostis* and the striking foliage species *S. pennata*. Both provide interest and beauty in the garden as well as being invaluable cut-foliage subjects.

However, of all the grasses my favourite must be the so-called hardy sugar cane, *Miscanthus sacchariflorus*. Of bamboo-like stature and appearance this is one of the most versatile grasses of all. It will grow in dryish garden soil, beside a pool or can be planted as a hedge or windbreak. There is a golden form called 'Aureus' and a striped leafed cultivar with green and white banded leaves known as 'Variegatus'.

SELECTED SUN LOVERS

There are so many old cottage garden favourites that fall into this category that it is difficult to know where to begin. So I propose to select those for which I have a strong affection and which embrace all seasons with their blossoms and yet at the same time have every prospect of prospering anywhere in the kingdom. So it is to the musk that I must first turn, a plant that epitomized cottage gardening in Victorian times, and yet a plant which today has left us with one of the greatest botanical and horticultural mysteries of all time. Just how did it lose its scent?

Musk and mimulus

The true musk, *Mimulus moschatus*, was grown extensively in cottage gardens by our grandparents for its delicious heady fragrance. Indeed, apart from being grown in the open garden it was raised in pots for the window ledge. Without its scent it would never have made any impact, for it is a rather uninspiring character which produces small mounds of greyish-green, pubescent foliage and rather inconspicuous yellow blossoms. Introduced by the plant collector Douglas in 1826 from western North America, it was grown in England, the seed yielding amongst many scentless plants one scented individual. It was this scented variation that was propagated and widely grown. In the early years of this century this fragrance mysteriously disappeared. There are a number of theories

Mixed borders ensure that there is year round interest, the shrubs
providing a framework around which border plants can be woven.

about this phenomenon, but one of the most frequently proposed is that the scented form broke down genetically. Although seed collected from the scented form always yielded scentless plants, some botanists believe that it is not beyond the bounds of possibility that by regularly raising *M. moschatus* from seed, a scented mutation will appear once again. Until that day we will have to rely upon other members of the family to provide us with garden worthy plants.

There are certainly plenty amongst the mimulus, popularly referred to as monkey musks. Especially the various strains and cultivars derived from the complex inter-crossing of *M. luteus*, *M. guttatus* and *M. cupreus*. These are numerous, and a detailed account of all that is available would be tedious. However, four selections are outstanding and deserve special mention. The vivid red 'Bonfire' and boldly spotted 'Queen's Prize' strains, together with the recently introduced hybrids 'Royal Velvet' and 'Yellow Velvet'. Both *M. luteus* and the closely allied *M. guttatus* are old friends, straggling stoloniferous perennials that are never more happy than when spreading around in wet soil at the poolside. Both have bright yellow blossoms, those of *M. guttatus* being spotted with red, while *M. luteus* sports golden flowers which are prominently etched with reddish-purple.

Mimulus cupreus is a smaller and more restrained character with orange-red flowers. A stunning contrast, and the parent of the most outstanding mimulus of all, the tiny 'Whitecroft Scarlet'. This is a little gem with neat mats of bright green foliage and small hooded blossoms of the brightest red.

Poppies and phlox
Poppies are plants that are always associated with cottage gardens, especially the giant oriental poppy, *Papaver orientale*. This is a tough resilient character that will flourish in almost any soil providing that it is in full sun. Attaining a height of a metre (yard) or more, the typical oriental poppy has dark red silky blossoms with a black centre.

These are held on hairy stems above coarse bristly foliage. The flowers are followed by handsome, pepper-pot seed heads which can be cut and dried for winter decoration. Cultivars of *P. orientale* are legion, but the double 'Salmon Glow', orange-scarlet 'Marcus Perry' and the single-flowered 'Perry's White' are all reliable. 'Allegro Vivace' is a dwarf red flowered kind with a dark centre that rarely grows more than 75 cm (2½ ft) high and one of the few poppies that comes absolutely true from seed. Unless you want mixed colours, seed raising is not a good idea. Root cuttings taken during the winter are the only way of successfully increasing named kinds.

Phlox can be increased in a similar way. Truly moisture-loving perennials, the various cultivars of the border phlox, *Phlox paniculata*, do best in a cool summer, but must be grown in the open if they are to flourish. Dependable sorts are 'Balmoral', lavender, 'Brigadier', red and 'White Admiral'. These all produce magnificent scented flower heads, unlike 'Norah Leigh' which is mostly cultivated for its variegated foliage; bright contrasting leaves on rather skinny stems, a plant that clearly does not belong in the cottage garden but which would like to suggest otherwise.

Daylilies certainly belong in the tangled informality of the mixed border, providing an excellent contrast to the later flowering phlox, but enjoying the same situation and soil conditions. These provide a marvellous display for much of the summer. Even though each individual blossom only lasts for a single day, there are so many that the show is continuous. Trumpet-shaped and carried amongst clumps of strap-shaped leaves, colours vary according to cultivar from deep purple-red through orange and yellow to pink. Try the old-fashioned *Hemerocallis lilio-asphodelus*, better known now as *H. flava*, with its clear yellow scented blossoms on wiry stems and carried amongst neat tufts of bright green foliage. Together with the richly fragrant citron-yellow, *H. citrina*, it makes a duo which for

Right: Oriental poppy, *Papaver orientale*, Queen of the summer border. Easily raised from seed and available in myriad colours from white and pink to scarlet.

Below: Plants of varieties both ancient and modern live happily together in this colourful border.

elegance and simplicity are unsurpassed by any of the modern cultivars.

Delphiniums and lupins

Delphiniums and lupins are great plants for a mixed border in an open sunny position, their bold spires or columns of blossoms having an architectural quality as well as contributing bright splashes of colour. Most of the popular delphiniums have been derived from *Delphinium elatum* and include cultivars like 'Blue Tit', the creamy-white 'Butterball' and purple-blue 'Cinderella'. When trying to reproduce a cottage garden atmosphere avoid the modern red and deep pink flowered cultivars as these look unnatural. In fact the most appropriate delphiniums of all are probably to be found in the so-called *belladonna* group, an array of shorter growing, smaller flowered hybrids, which although available in named varieties to colour, are equally satisfactory from a mixed seed selection. Like the *elatum* delphiniums, the belladonnas will require staking. The truly dwarf modern strains, such as 'Blue Fountains', although good modern garden plants, are not wholly in sympathy with our kind of gardening. At least not in the same way as lupins.

There are myriad named cultivars of lupins with colourful spires of striking pea-like flowers, but I would be just as happy with a mixed strain of Russell hybrids raised from seed – the most economical way of creating a colourful display quickly. Indeed, lupins often need replacing more regularly than you anticipate for they are very short-lived on dry soil. I like to incorporate plenty of organic matter into the soil before planting to improve its moisture-retaining properties. Adequate soil preparation before planting is vital as lupins resent disturbance and once planted remain in that position for the rest of their life.

Alstroemeria, scabious and pyrethrum

The same applies to the Peruvian lilies or alstroemeria. The best mixed strain called 'Ligtu Hybrids' has to be raised from seed started in pots and the young plants must be pot grown until planting out time. This does not apply to the commercial, cut-flower cultivar 'Dover Orange' whose rootstocks can often be purchased at the local market in regions with a strong horticultural tradition for a few pounds a bushel. One of the last products for which the bushel is used as a unit of volume! Flowering throughout the summer, alstroemeria produces large heads of brightly coloured, waxy, trumpet-shaped flowers on strong flower stems, that are first class for cutting.

Scabious is another jolly good cut flower that has been grown around country cottages for years. Particularly *Scabiosa caucasica* and its varieties. 'Clive Greaves' is a lovely lilac-blue and for many years has been grown in the fens for cut flower work. It is a lime-loving plant that must have a well-drained, open sunny position if it is to prosper. Known primarily as plant for the florist, the scabious nevertheless associates well with other herbaceous plants in the mixed border, its pale green leaves and soft lilac-blue flowers providing a cool contrast to the many other bright coloured border subjects. Flowering from mid-summer until mid-autumn, they are amongst the easiest of the border perennials to cultivate.

This could not be said of the pyrethrum. Although I love the simplicity and clear colours of the daisy-like blossoms of this charming plant, nothing will induce me to try growing it again. There can be no woman as fickle as a pyrethrum. Identical conditions on similar soils will yield different results and without any apparent reason. The same variety may be grown and one will sulk and suffer a lingering death, while its contemporary in the next garden will flourish and need regular division. Yet I am still bound to include them, for as woman is a vital ingredient in the life of man, so are pyrethrums in the cottage garden.

If you can grow them well they are a delight, but you will need a free-draining soil, an element of luck, and abundant

The use of ferns here is quite delightful, the handsome shield fern in the centre being particularly pleasing.

patience. There are many good cultivars, all with large daisy-like blossoms and bright green, much-divided foliage. Try the bright red 'Kelway's Glorious', and the deep pink 'Brenda'. 'Eileen May Robinson' is the one grown commercially for cut flowers. While easier to grow, I feel that it lacks a little of the class of the other cultivars.

Chrysanthemums, pinks and border carnations

Chrysanthemums are a complete contrast to pyrethrums in their culture, for nothing could be simpler or more rewarding to grow. These are not the chrysanthemums of the flower shows, but those derived from the hardy shasta daisy, *Chrysanthemum maximum*. These again are widely grown for cut flowers, especially the named varieties like 'Phyllis Smith' with its frilled single blossoms or the fully double white flowered 'Esther Read' and 'Wirral Supreme'. So well known are these latter two characters, that gardeners talk about them like old friends, using their cultivar names without ever needing to refer to them by their generic name. As cut flowers they are superb, as border plants they are equally fine providing that you remember to remove the faded blossoms in order to allow succeeding flushes of bloom to develop properly. Neglect in this respect will result in clusters of button-like flowers.

Flowering during mid-summer, they provide a useful lead into the autumn display of the Michaelmas daisies. More correctly called asters, cultivars derived from *Aster novi-belgii* and *A. novae-angliae* create a cavalcade of colour from late summer until mid-autumn. There are dwarf kinds like the lavender-mauve 'Audrey' which seldom exceed 30 cm (1 ft), while 'Harrington's Pink' and the lavender-blue 'Ada Ballard' are a metre (yard) or more high. Easily accommodated anywhere in the open, Michaelmas daisies suffer one indignity, and that is mildew. However, this can be easily controlled by regularly spraying with a fungicide containing benomyl, but it must

be done regularly throughout the growing season and not just when the disease appears.

Pinks and border carnations are easier to manage as long as they have a nice limy soil in which to grow. Under acid conditions they linger and die. All have grey-green foliage that forms neat rounded hummocks above which the sweetly scented, satiny blossoms are produced. The cultivars of both pinks and border carnations are numerous, but the best loved of the cottage garden kinds is the one called 'Mrs. Sinkins', a really fragrant old-fashioned sort with icy-white flowers. In strictly commercial terms 'Mrs. Sinkins' has been superseded by more compact cultivars like the salmon pink 'Doris' and her sisters, but the lure of nostalgia has ensured her continuance.

Evening primrose and bellflower

The continuance of the evening primrose *Oenothera biennis* is also assured, but on different grounds, for it is likely to become an important crop in the quest for vegetable oil. Its many relatives, too, are the subject of considerable research at present. A native of North America, *Oenothera biennis* is a bold upright plant with large rosettes of narrow lance-shaped leaves and loose terminal spikes of sweetly scented yellow flowers. These open during the evening and illuminate the border as daylight fades.

Oenothera lamarckiana is of similar habit with large yellow flowers and broad crinkly leaves. It is a variable plant which may be as little as 40 cm (1 ft 4 in) high or in excess of 90 cm (3 ft). Innumerable cultivars have been derived from this species, the most outstanding being 'Afterglow' and the sweetly scented 'Johnsonii'.

I always think that the border campanulas or bellflowers look good in the company of evening primroses. *Campanula persicifolia* is undoubtedly the best-loved of these, being a reliable plant of striking appearance with metre (yard) high spires of azure blooms. There are many cultivars from which to choose if you require something more sophisticated, but I like to stay with the single white 'Snowdrift' for variation in colour, but would go for the fully double 'Wirral Belle' for diversity of habit. When something really robust is required, plant *C. latiloba*. This is a very good plant for mixed shrubbery planting, although it always likes its head in the sun. 'Highcliffe Variety' is a trifle more refined and has silky upright bells of deep violet-blue. This deserves a prominent place towards the front of the border, perhaps adjacent to the snowy-white *C. l. alba*, presenting a perfect floral picture on a bright midsummer's day.

The towering powdery blue spikes of *C. lactiflora* appear at about the same time and command a position to the rear of the border. Here they can intermingle with the violet-blue 'Prichard's Variety' and pale blush 'Loddon Anna', or provide a foil for the diminutive 'Pouffe', an amicable dwarf with sky-blue blooms of conventional size.

Bearded iris

Finally in my selection of suitable cottage garden perennials I come to the bearded iris. Flag irises to some people, but whatever you call them they are that great group of lovely summer flowered irises derived from the bright purple-blue *Iris germanica* and the albino *I. florentina*; orris root of the herbalist and perfumer and *Fleur de Lis* of French heraldry. Both are strong rhizomatous perennials that are worth considering on their own account. They have deliciously fragrant blossoms and are of a strong constitution. *Iris florentina* I particularly favour, especially when planted in association with

the vivid orange Siberian wallflower, *Cheiranthus allionii*. The cultivars derived from these two iris species are numerous and include every colour of the spectrum. So any choice of cultivar is a very personal one. There are short growing kinds, taller ones and innumerable in-between sizes. Indeed, the consultation of a good grower's catalogue will spoil the gardener for choice. If possible take a look at the plants flowering in the nurseryman's field or visit one of the early summer flower shows and take your pick. Modern cultivars are especially weatherproof.

Unlike most other herbaceous plants, bearded or germanica irises are planted immediately after flowering. Established groups also require lifting and dividing every four or five years as their flowers fade. The stronger outside rhizomes are selected for replanting and the inner woody material is discarded. Any signs of softness in the rhizome should be carefully investigated. Irises suffer from a pernicious disease called rhizome rot which can decimate all the irises in the garden. Evidence of rotting, coupled with a sweet sickly smell, are characteristic of this disease which spreads quickly if no remedial action is taken. Cut or damaged surfaces of rhizomes should always be dressed with sulphur as this helps to seal the wound and ward off infection. Tall foliage must be reduced and the rhizome planted so that the top is just exposed. As all rhizomatous irises benefit from warm sunny conditions, the rhizomes are arranged as far as possible so that they point due south. The fan of leaves is then behind them and cannot shade the rootstock from the sun.

8

BULBS

Bulbs and herbaceous perennials are an integral part of any cottage garden. Indeed, it is they that largely create that indefinable quality which indicates to the casual observer that the garden is that of a cottager. It is not only the varieties of plants that are indicative of this special association, but their arrangement with one another. Even the fact that many old cottage garden cultivars have long since departed cannot impair the illusion created if careful selection is made amongst the wealth of modern varieties available. My selection here, of what it is appropriate to include in the cottage garden is purely personal. There are probably two or three times as many suitable kinds available which would create the desired effect as I have described. My judgement is based upon what I believe are other gardeners' expectations of what cottage garden plants should be and those that I have personally associated with such gardens over the past twenty-five years. So let us start with the spring flowering bulbs.

DAFFODILS AND TULIPS

Daffodils

Daffodils and tulips are amongst the most exciting and popular families of spring flowering bulbs. Known botanically as *Narcissus*, the daffodils and those popularly called narcissus, embrace a diversity of shape, form and size unequalled in the bulb kingdom. The newcomer to gardening is usually tempted by old well tried cottage garden types like 'Golden Harvest', 'King Alfred' and 'Carlton'. Cheap and cheerful kinds that give a dependable show with the minimum of effort. Commendable though they

are, these old stagers have been surpassed now by varieties like 'Rembrandt', 'Unsurpassable' and the quite startling sulphurous-yellow 'Spellbinder'. 'Ice Follies' dominates the creamy-white daffodil varieties, while 'Mrs. R. O. Backhouse' is a lovely shell pink and 'Texas' and 'Inglescombe' reliable double yellow sorts. For something out of the ordinary we must turn to the ever popular, fully double tazetta narcissus 'Cheerfulness', a richly fragrant kind with exotic-looking creamy blossoms. This can be grown outside successfully in most places, but is really a plant of the cottage window sill.

The various kinds that are loosely termed 'narcissus' by gardeners are those with broad flat faces and small brightly coloured trumpets. Indeed, one could say that 'Geranium' and 'Actaea' typify this class, although technically each belongs to its own division within the narcissus classification.

Apart from traditional daffodils and narcissus there are myriad dwarf varieties and species suitable for the rock garden, tubs or pots. Of these the most important are the dwarf trumpet kinds. Complete miniature replicas of the large flowered varieties and rarely exceeding 15 cm (6in) in height, they are usually represented by *Narcissus asturiensis* and *N. nanus*, or occasionally the lovely little Tenby Daffodil, *N. lobularis*. A complete contrast is provided by the hoop petticoats. Elegant creatures whose expanded globular trumpets dance and frolic in the breeze amongst narrow rushlike foliage. *Narcissus bulbocodium* typifies the hoop petticoat daffodil, but its many varieties, amongst them *conspicuus* and *citrinus*, produce blossoms of better substance and colour. Although popularly assigned to the rock garden both the hoop petticoats and cyclamen flowered narcissus are perfect for naturalizing in grass.

Despite the daffodil breeders having worked extensively with the *cyclamineus* narcissus, none of their efforts can compare with the charm and elegance exhibited by the true species, *N. cyclamineus*. Delicately sculptured blossoms, described most aptly by that great daffodil expert E. A. Bowles as having reflexed petals 'like the ears laid back of a kicking horse', are carried on slender stems scarcely 15 cm (6 in) high amongst a waving sea of grassy foliage. The advantage of growing *N. cyclamineus* is that it flowers so early. In favourable districts it will provide a show from early spring, a characteristic shared by its large flowered progeny, 'February Gold', 'Peeping Tom' and 'Jack Snipe', which makes them worth considering too. Indeed, these latter, apart from flowering early, remain in bloom for several weeks, particularly if grown in a semi-shaded location.

Angel's tears, *N. triandrus var. albus*, is not so amenable to cultivation in the open, although it will happily colonize a well-drained pocket on the rock garden. To see it to greatest advantage it should be grown in a pan in a cool place indoors where its creamy-white blossoms can be observed at eye-level. Varieties with shades that vary from off-white to rich golden-yellow are available as well as larger hybrids in which the *triandrus* character predominates. Most famous of these is the lovely cool icy-white 'Thalia'. Equally well loved, the jonquils comprise not only the renowned sweetly scented, old fashioned *N. jonquilla* with its myriad bright golden blossoms, but other interesting characters like the tiny *N. juncifolius* and its cousin *N. rupicola*. Both have richly scented short-cupped blossoms, deep green rush-like foliage, and an ability to flourish in our fickle climate.

Tulips

Tulips offer us an equal diversity, with some varieties flowering in early spring and others as late as early summer. Like narcissus, tulips fall into clearly defined groups, which although having no botanical significance, are widely accepted by gardeners to identify different kinds. Single early tulips are short growing kinds typified by the old fashioned 'Keizerskroon', the red and gold tulip of public conservatories and the forced bulb trade. While many of the more recent cultivars can equally be used for pot culture, they grow just as well outdoors. Flowering during mid-spring they are most frequently used for formal bedding rather than informal planting. Darwin tulips are later flowering and are used by parks' departments in their spring bedding schemes amongst forget-me-nots and wallflowers. 'Rose Copeland' has lovely blossoms of silvery-rose and carmine, while 'Princess Elizabeth' is pink and 'William Pitt' a vivid scarlet.

The union of Darwin and single early tulips has resulted in a group known as the Triumph tulips. These are very similar to Darwins, but flower much earlier and also have the shorter habit of the single earlies. Amongst these are well known kinds like 'First Lady', 'Merry Widow' and 'Edith Eddy'. Darwin tulips were also involved in the development of the Mendel tulips, a group of early flowering sorts which are excellent for indoor work. Grown outside they flower mid-spring and although good cultivars are limited, 'Apricot Beauty' and 'Pink Trophy' have always done well with me on a cold, uncompromising clay soil.

Cottage tulips extend the flowering season right up until early summer. A mixed blessing, for if the space that they are occupying is required for summer bedding plants they can be rather a nuisance. In the mixed border they are very useful, cultivars like the red and yellow 'Princess Margaret Rose' and pure white 'Maureen' giving a good account of themselves. There are also lily-flowered, fringed and viridiflora tulips, all with something to offer the cottage gardener, but of the less popular groups it is the parrot tulips that are the most appropriate. With frilled, flouncing blossoms those are best represented by 'Orange Favourite' and 'Texas Gold'.

Species tulips should not be overlooked by the cottage gardener, for these comprise a diversity of characters that can be accommodated in many parts of the garden. While correctly referring to wild species, in bulb merchants' terms the species tulips also include those cultivars directly attributable to a species. In recent years work with *Tulipa fosteriana*, *T. eichleri*, *T. kaufmanniana* and *T. greigii* have yielded a wealth of these, all neat, colourful and compact. *Tulipa kaufmanniana*, the waterlily tulip, has probably had the greatest influence, a charming little fellow with white or yellow blossoms heavily flushed with crimson or pink. *Tulipa eichleri* and *T. fosteriana* are brilliant scarlet, along with *T. greigii* which has handsome seagreen foliage splashed and streaked with purple. Consideration of the tulip species would not be complete, without the multiheaded *T. praestans*, an excellent tulip for heavy clay soils where it happily forms small colonies. Its cultivar 'Fusilier' is even more striking, producing groups of three or four vivid scarlet flowers on stout stems.

OTHER SPRING FLOWERING BULBS

Apart from narcissus and tulips there are a host of other equally worthy, spring flowering bulbs. Hyacinths for example, with their richly fragrant blossoms, each arranged with mathematical precision on short stout flower stems. Best suited to tubs and window boxes, hyacinths are available in a range of bright colours. 'Jan Bos' is red, 'Ostara' blue and 'L'Innocence' white; there are 'Yellow Hammer' and 'Pink Pearl' as well as the apricot-orange 'Cinderella'.

Crocuses provide a breath of spring, flowering in late winter if you choose *Crocus chrysanthus* cultivars. Smaller flowered than the usual sorts, these produce clusters of flowers from each corm. The yellow 'E. A. Bowles' and blue and white 'Ladykiller' are commonly grown, along with 'Zwanenburg Bronze' and 'Snow Bunting'. The large flowered or Dutch crocus rarely make a splash until mid-spring. Affectionately known as 'fat boys', these have shapely chalice-like blossoms in a wide array of colours. 'Remembrance', purple, 'Joan of Arc', white and the bright yellow 'Golden Mammoth' are amongst the most popular.

Snowdrops and winter aconites are offered for sale along with other spring flowering bulbs during the autumn. While it is perfectly reasonable to assume that one should plant them in their dormant state, it is in fact better to move them after flowering when still in a leaf. 'In green' is the term that the nurseryman uses to describe plants that are in such a state of preparedness. Spring flowering cyclamen, like the fragrant red *Cyclamen repandum* and red, pink or white *C. coum* should be similarly treated. If purchased as dry 'corms' in the autumn they are very reluctant to break dormancy.

There is no such problem with the early flowering glory of the snow, *Chionodoxa luciliae*. This is one of the easiest bulbs to grow irrespective of soil, producing masses of starry blue and white blossoms on short stems, amongst dark green, strap-like foliage. It needs careful placing though, for chionodoxa seeds readily and forms extensive colonies quite quickly. However, where it can be left to its own devices beneath trees and shrubs, it is an absolute joy.

Grape hyacinths also produce expansive colonies: great sheets of blue which, when planted beneath yellow flowered forsythia, present a picture of startling beauty. There are a number of different grape hyacinths, but all have typical clustered heads of tiny blue or white flowers which in the common *Muscari armeniacum* look just like tiny clusters of grapes. *Muscari botryoides* is pale blue and *M. comosum* 'Plumosum' has feathery flower heads of similar hue.

Bulbous iris flower about the same time as grape hyacinths, the cultivars of *Iris reticulata* being widely grown and quite outstanding. Rarely more than 10 cm (4 in) high and

Daffodils in the orchard herald the arrival of spring. Properly managed
they will become a permanent feature.

with long slender leaves they appear mostly in shades of blue. Both 'Joyce' and 'Harmony' are vigorous and increase freely. So does the plum coloured 'J. S. Dijt' and the white flowered *reticulata* type known as *I. vartani alba*. *Iris danfordiae* is like a bright yellow *I. reticulata*, but not very consistent in flowering. The first season is no problem, but then it breaks up into dozens of tiny bulbs which need at least a year to attain flowering size. It is prudent to plant *I. danfordiae* on a regular basis to ensure that at least one colony flowers. Some gardeners say that, by planting deeper than usual, larger bulbs persist and flower on a regular basis and this is certainly worth trying.

When choosing spring flowering bulbs, give due attention to those that I have just mentioned, but also take an excursion through the section in the bulb catalogue headed 'Miscellaneous Bulbs'. Here you will find not only *Chionodoxa*, *Crocus* and *Muscari*, but many easily grown subjects that extend from *Anemone* to *Zephyranthes*, many with cottage garden associations.

BULB SELECTION AND PLANTING

Always purchase your bulbs as early in the season as possible. The shapes of various bulbs are shown in Fig. 10. The sooner that they are planted the better. Bulbs that spend several weeks in polythene bags on the shelves of the local supermarket or garden centre are unlikely to be as successful as those purchased shortly after arrival from the grower and which have been stored in the cool of the nursery packhouse. Many of us have to resort to buying by mail order if there are special cultivars that we are seeking. This need not extend to the popular kinds though, and I would always advocate selecting your own bulbs whenever possible, carefully passing over any that are soft or discoloured.

With narcissus it is imperative to feel the base plate from around which the roots will emanate. If this is soft discard the bulb. Similarly avoid crocus or tulips that have lost their skins or tunics. These skins provide the bulbs with protection from all kinds

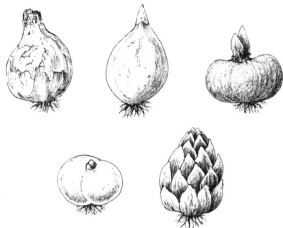

Fig 10. Popular bulbs and corms. *Top row: left to right:* Daffodil, tulip, crocus. *Bottom row:* Fritillary (*left*), lily.

of diseases and disorders. Naked bulbs are very vulnerable to rotting.

Snowdrops must be carefully inspected for signs of the devastating grey mould disease and the tiny bulbous iris must have clean white tunics. Black spots on the skins are a sign of the very contagious ink spot disease and it is wise to avoid purchasing even healthy looking iris from that source for the remainder of that season. Large bulbs of every variety, species or cultivar provide the best results, so always purchase the largest bulbs that you can afford. Multinosed narcissus are an excellent buy and if you want a good display of hyacinths settle for nothing less than the largest size.

Soil preparation

Correct soil conditions are essential, particularly in the case of tulips where free drainage is vital. Plenty of organic matter should be incorporated into the soil before planting, but this should not be fresh or unrotted manure. Slow acting fertilizers like bone meal and hoof and horn are ideal. Planting depths vary for the tuber, corm or bulb concerned, but in most cases twice

Naturalized bulbs are more in keeping with the cottage garden than those arranged in serried ranks in many suburban gardens.

their depth is the norm. That is the total depth of the bulb is the depth of the covering of soil above the nose. This is not a universal rule, for hardy cyclamen are planted at soil level, but it applies to most subjects. Some gardeners maintain that bulbs should be planted at two or three times the diameter of the bulb, but this is more difficult to gauge. Recent experiments with narcissus and tulips also suggest that they at least benefit from deeper planting than hitherto recommended.

Bulb planting

Always use a trowel to plant rather than a dibber, unless you have very light sandy soil. When pushed into heavy soil, a dibber leaves a pointed depression into which the bulb rests, but also leaves a small air pocket beneath the bulb which quickly fills with water and will cause rots to set in. Proper bulb planting trowels are especially useful, being narrow bladed and having various planting depths inscribed upon the face. With the aid of one of these, the correct depth can easily be achieved, a vital factor when planting a bedding scheme in which the tulips must all be of uniform height. Formal bedding ideas demand great accuracy with planting and a measuring stick and line are essential, additional aids.

In the cottage garden bulbs are often naturalized, especially narcissus. In order to create the natural look scatter the bulbs gently by hand over the area intended for planting and then plant them in the positions in which they have fallen. When planting in established lawn or grassland, the soil beneath is likely to be compacted. This should be loosened with a fork and plenty of sharp sand or grit incorporated, to the benefit of both turf and bulbs. It is best not to plant through the sward; lift the turf, plant the bulbs and then replace. This allows you to prepare the soil much more satisfactorily than poking about in a hole through the turf. Even more preferable, plant bulbs in well prepared and cultivated soil, sowing grass on the top after planting.

THE AFTERCARE OF BULBS

If you select good-sized bulbs of first-class quality during the autumn you can almost guarantee a good show the following spring. After that it is up to you to maintain this quality in the planted bulbs in order to secure succeeding displays of flowers. For top quality blossoms it is essential to have the bulbs growing in soil that is in good heart. Those that are going to be of long standing must also be fed regularly, either with a generous spring application of bonemeal or a liquid feed after flowering while the leaves are still healthy and green. Liquid feed needs careful application in order to prevent rapid foliage development and the production of soft bulbs which will succumb to moulds and rots during the winter.

Providing that competition from weeds and other neighbouring plants is kept to a minimum, the production of good sized healthy bulbs is almost assured. That is providing that you maintain the foliage for as long after flowering as possible. The function of bulb foliage at this time is to develop the bulb for the next season and ensure the initiation of lower buds. By the time that the leaves have died down next spring's flowers should be latent within the bulbs. No amount of feeding or replanting at this time will have any effect. Unsightly bulb foliage is usually a constant source of irritation after all the flowers have faded as it begins to look jaded and unhealthy. However it is vital that it remains for at least six weeks after flowering, preferably until it disappears of its own accord, in order to build up the food reserves in each bulb.

Some gardeners lift, divide and store their bulbs, replanting in the autumn. This is unnecessary unless you want to fill the gaps that they leave with summer bedding or hardy annuals. In that case the bulbs will still be in leaf, so lift carefully and line them out in another part of the garden until all the foliage has died back naturally. Then is the time to lift, dry and sort them prior to storing in a cool dry place. Apart from tulips, I would seldom contemplate the disturbance of healthy bulbs unless it was clear that they had been in position for many years and were in desperate need of dividing and replanting.

The potential bare patches created by bulbs which are dying back can be filled with some of the hardy annuals if the seed is scattered amongst the receding foliage. Cornflower, night scented stock, Virginian stock, clarkia and godetia all hide the foliage well and their growth is not impeded by its presence. Remember that these annuals will take nourishment from the soil in which the bulbs are growing and so take appropriate measures with bonemeal or hoof and horn during the early spring.

SUMMER-FLOWERING BULBS

Most gardeners assume that bulbs are only planted during the autumn, except perhaps for lilies and gladioli. This is rather sad as there are numerous colourful kinds which can be planted during the spring for summer flowering. We seem to have forgotten many of the very beautiful and easily cultivated kinds which our grandparents used to grow and which were often seen in cottage gardens. Crocosmia for example, the genus which now embraces the garden montbretias, the name *Montbretia* only being appended to a rather rare and unusual plant known as *Montbretia laxiflora*.

Garden montbretias are now all technically derived from *Croscosmia crocosmiiflora*, apparently a union between *C. aurea* and *C. pottsii*. Many cultivars are available, including the lemon-yellow 'Citronella' and orange-scarlet 'His Majesty'. Regarded as traditional cottage garden plants, the modern named cultivars are not as invasive as their forebears and can be relied upon to behave themselves rather better than those that granny used to grow. Unlike many of the bulbs recommended for spring planting,

the corms of crocosmia are very hardy and can remain in the soil through the winter.

So can the strange little rootstocks of the old fashioned turban ranunculus. Although neither bulb, corm nor tuber, their strange little claw-like rootstocks are dealt with by the bulb trade. Being unlike anything else the gardener is likely to encounter, these weird rootstocks cause considerable confusion as to which way up they should be planted. Always bury them just beneath the soil surface with the points of the claws downwards. Turban ranunculus produce spreading divided foliage, not unlike that of the common buttercup. Also beautiful double silky blossoms in a wide range of bright colours on stems that are long enough for cutting.

Anemones can also be used for cutting, especially the semi-double 'St. Brigid' and single 'De Caen' strains. These are in myriad bright colours and can be planted at regular intervals to ensure a succession of blossoms. Specialist bulb suppliers sometimes list both 'De Caen' and 'St. Brigid' anemones by cultivar names. When available these should be sought out for they are really superb. The rich purple-blue 'Mr. Fokker' and fiery red 'Hollandia' I always associate with old fashioned gardens. The black or brown raisin-like rootstock known popularly as a corm, is botanically a tuber and by virtue of this fact is able to expand in the soil. So once you plant anemones they are a permanent and developing feature. Persuading them to sprout in the first place can be difficult unless you soak them in water overnight. All the sound tubers are planted about 2.5 cm (1 in) beneath the surface of the soil. The flowering period can be extended from late spring until early autumn with successional plantings.

Gladioli

I mentioned gladioli earlier as being popular summer flowering bulbs, but the large brash cultivars that are produced nowadays are totally out of context when planted in a cottage garden. The early flowered *nanus* group are much more evocative of days gone by. Popularly known as *Gladiolus colvillei* and named after the Chelsea nurseryman who first popularized them, they are available in a wide range of pastel colours and are all of modest stature, mixing well in the herbaceous or mixed border.

Having tried many cultivars I always return to the old faithful 'Nymph'. This seems to have far more blossoms for a greater period of time than any other hybrid. It is excellent for cutting, with beautifully sculptured white blossoms with crimson shading. 'Blushing Bride' looks very similar, but is not as free with its favours. Nor is the pure white 'The Bride' which although vigorous, never yields the same quantity of blossoms as 'Nymph'. 'Ackerman' is an old cultivar with orange-red flowers, while those of 'Amanda Mahy' are deep pink with mauve internal splashes. 'Peach Blossom' is an exceptional pink cultivar, which although aged, had yet to be surpassed in its own colour range.

All the *G. colvillei* types flower from midsummer onwards outdoors, although it is possible for the enthusiastic gardener to plant the corms in pots during the autumn, giving them cool greenhouse cultivation until the spring when they will come into flower. While delightful for such an enterprise, I feel that they are really much more at home in the tangled informality of a mixed border in a cottage garden.

Lilies

Lilium is a diverse group of plants, mostly summer flowering, and are often regarded by the newcomer to gardening as exotic looking and therefore probably temperamental. There are a few that live up to this reputation, but the majority of the popular garden varieties are easily satisfied if given a little shade and a moisture-retentive soil which does not become waterlogged during winter. Lilies are planted from late autumn onwards, although the majority of bulbs will be seen in garden shops during early spring.

It is important that when buying bulbs

that you only purchase from a retailer who is looking after the bulbs properly. They should be stored in boxes of peat or wood shavings, never exposed to the desiccating effect of warm dry air. Except, of course, for the Queen of the cottage garden, the lovely pure white flowered Madonna lily, *Lilium candidum*. Unlike its cousins, this species must be planted before the end of the summer in order to be able to produce its overwintering rosette of foliage.

When grown amongst other plants lilies rarely require staking as their flowering stems are usually very vigorous and sturdy. Only really large flowered kinds like the golden-rayed lily of Japan, *Lilium auratum* and the regal lily, *L. regale*, are likely to need a stout support. In my view neither of these really belong in a cottage garden if one views the concept purely aesthetically. Factually, however, it remains true that both were to be seen in country gardens shortly after the turn of the century. I feel that the modern 'Mid-Century' hybrids are much more in keeping with the atmosphere which we are trying to create even though some of the colours may be rather brash. They are all easy-going as well and ask for little more than a friable moisture-retentive soil. Likewise that true cottage garden favourite *L. tigrinum*, the vivid orange tiger lily. I love this robust fellow with its seemingly perpetual show of spotted orange blossoms in late summer and those marvellous little bulbils which cluster in the leaf axils all the way up the stem, and if detached and planted, rapidly form a green forest of baby 'tigers'.

Few pests and diseases afflict lilies that are being grown in a well-nourished, free-draining soil. Virus is the likeliest problem to arise, causing flower contortion and the stunting of foliage. Unfortunately there is no cure for this malady and afflicted bulbs are best consigned to the bonfire. Periodically established clumps of lilies require lifting and dividing. This should be done in early spring just as the bulbs are starting into growth. Discard old misshapen bulbs and replant only young vigorous stock.

Clever planting with taller subjects visually reduces the height of the
cottage which more readily conforms with its surroundings.

9

HERBS AND FRAGRANT PLANTS

Fragrance should be as much a part of the garden as colour, the blending and isolating of scents being as important as the mixing and matching of different hues. A host of opportunities present themselves to the cottage gardener who is aware of the diversity of plant scents that there are and the effect that their careful use can have upon his chosen planting arrangement. If you look at the diversity of plants grown in cottage gardens it becomes quickly apparent that the majority had scented leaves or blossoms. We must now take a look at some of the subjects that were once so successfully grown and see how we can incorporate them into the general garden scene.

Cherry pie or heliotrope, *Heliotropium peruvianum*, is a fragrant delight from the past. A tender dwarf shrubby plant with pleasant foliage and corymbs of pale purple, sweetly scented flowers. The fragrance of heliotrope is difficult to define, being spicy, yet sweet, like the mixture of lavender and roses which small boys associate with grannies. Usually treated as an annual, heliotrope is easily raised from an early sowing of seed under glass, or alternatively cuttings taken during late summer can be over-wintered with protection.

Rosemary, *Rosmarinus officinalis*, is another old favourite, and justifiably so, a shrubby plant with narrow grey-green leaves that impart a rich fragrance. During summer its spire-like branches are sprinkled with delicate soft blue blossoms. There are both pink and white flowered forms as well as the fastigiate 'Miss Jessup'. This is the sturdy upright grower with the shape and habit of a small conifer which I suggested in an earlier chapter as a useful component of the mixed internal hedge. Rosemary enjoys a warm sunny position in a free-draining soil. While sometimes cut back severely during a hard winter, it will usually refurnish itself quite quickly.

The lemon balm, *Melissa officinalis*, can also be subject to winter damage, unless the old stems are left on the plants during the autumn. These can be removed when the worst of the frost is over. Treat balm like a hardy fuchsia and there will be no problems. Lemon balm is a herbaceous perennial which grows up to 75 cm ($2\frac{1}{2}$ ft) high, with dark green nettle-like foliage amongst which myriad tiny white blossoms are produced. There are several golden-leaved kinds, of which 'Aureus' is the most handsome, all with a heady lemon fragrance.

Lavender is another old fashioned plant which must be considered. Not just the *Lavandula spica*, but some of its named varieties. All have a neat habit that is well suited to the smaller garden, yet have lost none of the character which makes them so much a part of the cottage garden. 'Munstead', or 'Munstead Dwarf' is the most versatile, and excellent for internal hedging as well as integrating in the mixed border. The great advantage of this particular cultivar is that it can be raised evenly and easily from seed. 'Twickel Purple', and most of the others must be propagated from short summer cuttings. This is a cultivar with deep purple spires of flowers that contrast strongly with its grey-green foliage. Those of *var. alba* are pure white. Both are of compact habit and easily accommodated, unlike the bold shrubby 'Grappenhall Variety' which needs plenty of space in order to develop.

Fig. 11 shows the procedure involved in propagating from softwood cuttings.

HERBS

Thyme, sage and basil

Herbs always figure prominently when fragrant plants are considered. Thymes like the gorgeous caraway-scented, *Thymus herba-barona* and the lemon scented *T. citriodorus*. This latter is especially good in its golden-leaved form 'Aureus'. They are ideal for growing on low walls or in the niches of crazy paving, provided that they are not subjected to heavy foot traffic. Their clusters of pinkish-mauve blossoms are a bonus. although not especially handsome, they do attract the attention of bees and thus give the planting a further dimension.

When thinking of herbs do not overlook the sages. Apart from the common sage, *Salvia officinalis*, and its coloured-leaved cultivars, there are other richly fragrant salvias which seldom receive the attention that they deserve. The pineapple sage, *S. rutilans*, is the one with the greatest appeal. A somewhat ungainly plant that is only hardy in favoured localities. It is often treated as a pot plant, although it grows well as a temporary inhabitant of the border. Young shoots taken as cuttings during late summer root quickly and provide sizeable plants that can be satisfactorily over-wintered in a frost-free place. It is an exciting plant with a delicious pineapple fragrance and spires of slender scarlet flowers during late summer.

The majority of salvias have aromatic foliage and a number possess flowers that have a hint of fragrance too. *Salvia aurea*, for example, a lovely plant with foliage that imparts a distinctive cucumbery tang. An amiable character of neat shrubby habit, it has bright primrose flowers which age to rich tawny brown and persist in their dried state for several weeks. Of similar disposition to the pineapple sage, this can be easily over-wintered as rooted cuttings or raised each year from seed sown inside during early spring.

Indeed, many of the culinary herbs are easy to raise this way. Essentially utility plants they are wonderful additions to the

Fig 11. Softwood cuttings.

(*a*) Remove a cutting from healthy non-flowering wood.

(*b*) Cut just bewneath a leaf joint.

(*c*) Remove the lower leaves.

(*d*) Dip the base of the cutting in hormone-rooting powder.

(*e*) Insert the cutting in a suitable rooting medium.

garden, providing not only flavouring for the kitchen, but adding scent and character as well. Some need the further protection of a cloche or frame in the early stages of growth. Those like the bush and sweet basils, *Ocimum minimum* and *O. basilicum*, which are sown during spring and given shelter until mid-summer. Unless you really must have sweet basil, then do not bother growing it, for it is an open gawky plant of unpredictable temperament that cannot be relied upon. Put your trust in the compact bush basil. This has smaller leaves, but these are regularly produced and have the same marvellous aroma of burning incense that the true basil has.

Of contrasting nature but easily seed raised, is the common borage, *Borago officinalis*, a large coarse character with rosettes of hairy leaves and stiff spikes of brilliant blue flowers. Apart from providing delicious young foliage for salads and blossoms for fruit cups, it is a plant of outstanding beauty and well able to hold its own in the herbaceous border. Seed sown during spring in the open ground produces plants of flowering size by mid-summer. These seed and provide a permanent stock of youthful plants. Truly biennial, the borage is a permanent fixture once in a situation to its liking, self-seeding freely and on occasion making itself a nuisance.

Angelica, chervil and parsley

This is not a problem with the most fickle of herbs, angelica, *Angelica archangelica*. A broad spreading leafy plant with white umbels of parsley-like flowers on towering stems more than a metre (yard) high. Treat angelica like a biennial. Allow it to flower and enjoy its bridal white blossoms in company with all the bees in the neighbourhood. If you are really interested in using the stem for candying rather than growing the plant for its architectural qualities, then remove the flower stalk before the bees have done their work. In this way the plant will remain perennial. Obviously if you are going to enjoy the great spreading plate-like blos-

soms, fresh plants will be required, and these are best raised from seed gathered as soon as ripe and sown directly in a soil-based compost. Germination will then be prolific and rapid. Purchased angelica seed sometimes gives results, but more often than not, disappointment.

Chervil, *Anthriscus cerefolium*, is another closely related herb of biennial habit. Some gardeners even regard it as an annual, although I have never had such experience. Allegedly tender in the early stages of growth, I have never experienced any difficulty in raising young plants in seed trays on the window ledge, transferring them to individual peat pots as soon as large enough to handle, and then planting outside during early summer. The foliage is pale green and fernlike, providing a useful fragrant foil for small, brightly coloured flowers at the front of the border. It is also used for garnishing in much the same manner as parsley and where difficulty is experienced in getting the latter established, makes a refreshing and amenable substitute.

With many gardeners of my acquaintance there is no greater aim in their horticultural life than to successfully raise a patch of common parsley, *Petroselinum crispum*. Some seem capable of growing it at will, while others resort to all manner of dubious methods to induce it to prosper. Soaking the seed in warm water and planting at the rising of the new moon are two of the more popular methods popularly advocated by disillusioned gardeners of my acquaintance. I believe that patience is the primary ingredient of success, although freshness of seed has a considerable bearing.

Parsley may take eight weeks to germinate, so it is essential to sow it in a relatively weed-free area of the garden. With taking so long to germinate, it will often rot before emerging on heavy clay soil. Therefore it is useful to sow the seeds in a good soil-less compost in a frame, pricking the seedlings out into individual small pots prior to planting. It is reputed amongst old cottage gardeners that transplanting parsley leads to an

Herbs and aromatic plants lessen the harshness of the stone paving, which
itself restricts the more invasive subjects.

addition to the family, so this method may well require a degree of caution!

Fennel, hyssop and marjoram

Fennel, *Foeniculum vulgare*, with its feathery green foliage and golden flowers is a striking perennial for the mixed border. Its graceful feathery foliage, especially in the bronze-leaved form, provides a perfect foil for the delicate blossoms of pinks and carnations. Traditionally used exclusively in fish dishes, my family enjoy the aniseed tang of its foliage chopped fresh and green in salads. Seed sown in its permanent position in a sunny open situation during early spring rapidly provides healthy vigorous plants. An average family's needs are provided by two or three plants, but I always raise more as the green foliage is so useful for blending in with the pastel shades of may border plants.

Hyssop, *Hyssopus officinalis*, responds to similar growing conditions but provides a very different kind of plant. The common hyssop is an attractive blue-flowered, broad-leaved shrub no more than 60 cm (2 ft) high, but there is also a smaller rock hyssop, *H. aristatus*, which is a complete dwarf, rarely more than 30 cm (1 ft) tall, which can be grown in a pot on the kitchen window ledge. I like to see them in the garden as they attract so much insect life, especially bees and butterflies. I must confess that I have never tried to make tea with their foliage, which I understand is the reason that the herb enthusiast grows them. Let us get our tea from India and China and leave these little chaps alone; they are first rate plants for the front of the border.

The various marjorams are also shrubby and should be treated rather like hyssop, except that you will find their foliage is rather unruly in comparison. There is quite a lot of confusion amongst the various marjorams as to which is which. If we add to that the fact that the Latin name of marjoram is *Origanum* and that marjoram and oregano are the same thing, then you will perhaps permit me a short dissertation to sort things out. Three species are commonly grown by gardeners, but it is the short growing, perennial pot marjoram *Origanum onites*, that I believe to be the most useful, even if allegedly the least tasteful. Sweet marjoram, *O. marjorana*, is the one for garnishing, but rather temperamental and usually treated as an annual, while wild marjoram, *O. vulgare*, is as its name suggests a trifle unruly for anywhere but the wild patch in the cottage garden. A roguish old perennial, it is this that posh folks refer to as oregano. I would never consider picking its leaves or shoots as they are sparse and spidery. In any case if you grow *O. vulgare* you will want to enjoy its purplish flowers, one of the greatest bee attractants that I know; not that bees are uninfluenced by the other two, for they both yield similar blossoms. I favour the pot marjoram above the others for its neatness of habit and winter reliability, when given a well-drained spot.

Rue, tarragon and mint

Rue, *Ruta graveolens*, has a smarter appearance than any of the marjorams and deserves a place for its colourful foliage alone. A semi-evergreen it has bluish-green, almost metallic leaves, which impart a rather strange and acrid aroma. Some find this pleasant, others objectionable. Rue produces tiny four-petalled yellow blossoms followed by strange little seed capsules which yield viable seed. This is the easiest way of increasing this little fellow, even the bizarre, cream-variegated form coming absolutely true. Sown with a little protection during early spring, plants will be ready for planting out during mid-summer and will start making an impression by the autumn. Apart from the ordinary and variegated types there is a selected foliage form, called 'Jackman's Blue' which has to be increased from cuttings.

The same applies to French tarragon, another strangely confused plant of the herbalist. Owing to the fact that French tarragon does not set seed freely in this

Bronze fennel and sorrel hold their own in this mixed flower border,
providing an interesting foil for colourful flowers.

country, if ever at all, all stock must be procured from cuttings. This ensures that you have the real thing with the wholesome flavour and distinctive fragrance; unlike the common Russian tarragon, which is raised from seed and produced in large quantities, to be rejected as an inferior subject for culinary purposes. What baffles me about this situation is that both are botanically the same plant, *Artemesia dracunculus*, but from different geographical locations. I cannot disprove the flavour theory nor would I wish to do so here, for our concern is more with the visual and fragrant aspects of the garden and for this purpose either stock will do. Both have the same visual attributes of being rarely more than 75 cm (2½ ft) high with fine green or green-grey foliage with occasional forked ends and spires of gritty nondescript flowers. Visually speaking, I would always go for the Russian strain as it is easily seed raised, a much more substantial plant and generally better looking.

There are numerous mints from which to choose, but all need treating with more than a little respect. They are invasive plants that readily swamp all their neighbours if afforded such a freedom. Most gardeners restrict them to a bucket or similar container sunk up to the rim in the soil. While in the short term this can be most effective, it can be destructive if the plants are not regularly lifted and divided, or increased from cuttings and all the soil in the container discarded.

The cause of all this activity is the likely presence of the deadly mint rust, a troublesome disease which causes devastation amongst both culinary and decorative mints. Spraying with a fungicide can control this menace, but the most reliable way of excluding it is to transfer vigorous young stock to fresh soil every couple of years. Good soil conditions and uncrowded growth seem to help in maintaining healthy plants. If rust should strike, and it looks exactly as the named describes it, remove all the aerial parts of the plant and then lift some of the runners. Ensure that these have no vestige of foliage attached able to carry infective spores, wash clean of all soil and replant. The resulting plants should be healthy, as the disease appears not to attack underground runners and is only specific to mint, with no alternative over-wintering host.

There are a number of different varieties of mint to choose from, the common green mint, *Mentha viridis*, being the most essential for the kitchen, and if allowed to flower, quite acceptable in the garden. There is spearmint, *M. spicata* and peppermint, *M. piperata*, each with foliage of a greenish hue. Also apple mint, *M. rotundifolia*, with handsome woolly foliage and the appropriately named eau-de-Cologne mint, *M. citrata*. This latter is most attractive, having low branching stems and roughly oval, somewhat oily, dull green leaves edged with purple which fill the air with a delicious fragrance on a warm sultry day. There are ginger, citrus and pineapple mints amongst the vast mint kingdom, all with something to offer, also pennyroyal, *M. pulegium*. Not a mint in the usual sense of the word, but a delightful small fragrant paving plant with small oval leaves and numerous whorls of tiny mauve flowers with a sweet and heady fragrance.

OTHER FRAGRANT PLANTS

Well, I think that we have had our fill of herbal plants, so just before we leave this chapter, which could so easily turn into a book itself, I must direct your attention to one or two old friends which could not be excluded from the cottage garden on any grounds. All hold happy childhood memories for me and would be an integral part of my cottage garden. The two for which I hold the fondest memories are the musky scented mignonette, *Reseda odorata*, and the sweet, sugary, sweet violet, *Viola odorata*. Neither are outstanding in their floral beauty, but both are essentially a part of a fragrant corner.

Right: Only with herbs can formality be permitted in a cottage garden. Here is a splendid example that is both decorative and functional.

Below: A vegetable garden has always been an integral part of the cottage garden. Although usually separated from the decorative garden, as here, some gardeners used to accommodate more ornamental crops like beetroot and runner beans in amongst the flowers.

I know that I have already waxed lyrical about sweet violets, but I must repeat their virtues here. They are first class easy-going plants that demand nothing more than a weed-free site on which to prosper. I have vivid memories of my aunt's garden, where beneath white lilac a green carpet spread itself, sprinkled with blossoms of violets, the almost unseen source of the sweet fragrance that mystified passersby on the other side of her picket fence. Mignonette does not provide such permanent fragrance as it is sadly of annual duration and in need of constant replacement; not the sort of plant to be included in a bedding scheme either, as its blossoms are of a not particularly endearing greenish-yellow hue.

In the cottage garden it is best in the mixed or herbaceous border, imparting its fragrance amongst brightly coloured neighbours. Mignonette is amenable to pot culture and traditionally a cottage window sill plant, a rather odd pot plant that has memories for me of a white thatched cottage, where my brother and I visited two old spinster sisters and ate quantities of a trifle called 'Glim-glom' as they regaled us with stories of the Indian Raj. Sown with protection during early spring its fragrance can be enjoyed for most of the summer.

Finally some shrubs of recent vintage, certainly not members of the cottage garden fraternity, for they were not around at that time. However, they all blend into the scene and I believe deserve every consideration. The first is the southern European and north African native *Cytisus battandieri*; a handsome fragrant shrub attaining a height of 3–4 m (10–13 ft) in a favourable situation, producing dense clusters of bright yellow flowers with a rich pineapple fragrance amongst silky grey-green foliage. Winter fragrances can be provided by *Viburnum farreri*, the *V. fragrans* of my childhood garden, and its modern progeny *V. bodnantense*. Both flower from early winter until late spring, their naked branches sprinkled with sweetly scented blossoms. *Viburnum farreri* has clusters of creamy-white flowers with a hint of green, while those of *V. bodnantense* are pink. Excellent for cutting, they can be conveniently pruned while flowering, although only large rooms can accommodate their overpowering fragrance.

Used at their most successful, scents and aromas are scattered about the garden. When grown in isolation they can be savoured, when grown together they mask one another and very often create a sickly pot-pourri.

10
WILD FLOWERS

Growing native wild flowers in the garden sounds very easy, for theoretically all that needs to be done is to allow a corner of the garden to return to nature. As with many theories the practical applications are fraught with difficulties. Allowing formerly cultivated land to return to a natural state does not work. Indeed, land that has been cultivated rarely returns to anything resembling that from which it was taken. All that happens is that pernicious annual weeds like groundsel and shepherds' purse take over, to be followed by one or more troublesome perennial kinds such as couch grass or bindweed. A proper wild flower area needs creating, for remember that the soil and situation are totally artificial and the climate is very unreal. Buildings create wind tunnels and swirls untypical of nature and the soil in which wild flowers grow successfully has rarely received fertilizer whether natural or artificial. It also follows that if an area has to be created for such plants, then they are unlikely to prosper without regular maintenance.

Deciding upon the kind of wild flowers that are to be grown depends very much upon climatic conditions and soil type. Correct acidity or alkalinity is just as critical with wild flowers as it is with cultivated ones. In fact it is essential to regard any wild area of the garden as any other part both in planning and maintenance. With planning I think that it is vital to have self-disciplining guide lines in order that it fulfils its purpose. It should be realized that such noble efforts in the cultivation of wild flowers are not conserving native plants in the way that we might think, for the serious student of the British flora requires material of known geographical location and genetic origin to be able to undertake worthwhile scientific research. Unless it is taken into account that by these plants currently being available for gardeners to buy, that they satisfy a long felt need formerly met by gathering material from the wild. The current trend in wild-flower cultivation seems to have little to do with conservation, it has arisen primarily through nostalgia for the country flowers of childhood, which under motorway construction and grass verge spraying have been drastically reduced. Therefore we have developed this strong desire to see snowdrops peeping through a mantle of snow and primroses winking from the base of the hedgerows. This is, of course, nothing new. It is just that the nursery trade would have us think so.

For many years cottage gardeners nurtured the jewels of the countryside. Even in my youth I can recall visiting a country cottage garden where part of the lawn was always allowed to remain untouched and where spotted orchids grew. To reinforce the importance of these orchids to us all I was told to look at the spots of Christ's blood on the foliage. I was informed that if I disturbed them I would be subject to the wrath of the Virgin Mary. A fanciful story, but one which shows how strongly country folk still regard the choicer wild flowers that grow around them. The same man would, without hesitation slash ground elder and brambles to the ground and then attack their roots with a mattock. There are native plants and native plants. The line must be drawn very carefully.

The pasque flower, *Pulsatilla vulgaris*, is one of the most glamorous and best loved of our native wild flowers, with blossoms like delicate purple goblets smothered in silky golden hairs which glisten in the sunshine. Naturally an inhabitant of thin, dry, calcareous soils, the pulsatilla enjoys nothing better than an open dry site in a good loam soil liberally mixed with limestone chippings. It is an easy-going subject once established, but does not transplant readily from open ground. This means that pot grown plants are essential. These can either be raised from seed or root cuttings. For the most part seed is quite satisfactory, particularly if it can be gathered fresh. This should be sown immediately in a John Innes compost and will germinate freely. As soon as large enough to handle, the seedlings should be potted individually.

The snakeshead lily, *Fritillaria meleagris*, could be regarded as an equal with the pasque flower in the popularity stakes. A bulbous subject, this has delicate chequered blossoms in shades of purple or pink and slender grassy foliage of a soft glaucous hue. One of the finest harbingers of spring, its natural haunts are damp meadows and woodland fringes where it rapidly forms sizeable colonies. So, when planted in the garden, a moist position amongst shrubs or in irregularly mown grass suits it well. Bulbs usually come to hand during late summer or early autumn. The tiny bulbs appear scaleless, but in fact consist of two or three fleshy scales which if exposed to the air for any time shrivel and die. Rough handling of the bulb and subsequent storage leads to moulds developing. This points to early autumn planting if they are to become quickly and successfully established.

Snakeshead lilies are typical meadowland flowers, and although it may be thought that meadowland conditions are likely to be the easiest to provide, they are in fact very difficult, especially when dealing with plants of annual duration. The grass in the area must be allowed to develop and remain uncut until the meadow flowers have ripened and cast their seed. If not carefully managed this can lead to the lodging of the grasses, the accumulation of thatch at their base, and subsequently little opportunity for the seeds to fall on suitable moist soil. Initial sowing in established grass areas should only be undertaken when the grass has been cut short and all the thatch or accumulated debris has been raked out to reveal bare areas of moist soil for seed contact. This then gives a reasonable opportunity for a hay meadow site to be recreated.

Mixed wild flower seed collections are available from a number of specialist seedsmen, some of whom have studied the subject and can offer you really good advice about the species most suited to your conditions. You can try a mixture and see which prospers, but I would rather pick one or two good reliable kinds out – well-known country flowers like the corncockle, *Agrostemma githago*, devil's bit scabious, *Succisa pratensis* or the field forget-me-not, *Myosotis arvensis*. Then there is the scarlet pimpernel, *Anagallis arvensis*, corn marigold, *Chrysanthemum segetum* and the tiny harebell, *Campanula rotundifolia*. All these are good on most soils and can be relied upon to flourish in an unkempt sward. It is not my favourite way of growing them, even though they are in their natural environment. How much better to cultivate them amongst other cottage garden flowers. As long as seeding is controlled they rarely become a nuisance and they add so much by way of colour and character, and being native they are quite reliable.

Wherever I eventually planted primroses, I would ensure that the site was properly prepared and the plants raised in the conventional way. True primroses, *Primula vulgaris*, are an absolute delight, but need proper conditions if they are to flourish. Sow the seed during mid-summer and raise the plants in trays or pots ready for planting out the following spring. In their early stages of growth primroses benefit from a little shading. They always require a constant supply of moisture and watering needs carefully attending to until they are well established, afterwards they look after themselves. The only time that anything needs to be done is when flower size and

Marsh marigolds, *Caltha palustris*, announce the arrival of spring. One of the most decorative plants for the natural garden.

A thatched cottage in a perfect setting. Old fashioned flowers in tangled
profusion, the rich scent of honeysuckle filling the air.

quantity start to diminish and the clumps begin to look congested. Division is then necessary, it most usefully being done immediately after flowering as with garden polyanthus, the young rooted pull-offs being planted back in suitably enriched soil.

The same can be done with the cowslip, *P. veris* and the oxslip, *P. elatior*, although these tend to enjoy more open situations. I find them all very amenable to border cultivation where they also seed themselves freely. Cowslips and oxslips look excellent in bold groups on their own, but primroses are at their best when peeping through a carpet of sweet violets, *Viola odorata*.

Wild strawberries, *Fragaria vesca*, are great fun to grow, delighting children who love to hunt through the dense carpet of foliage for tiny sweet red fruits. These are usually stolen by the birds and of marginal interest, but the white blossoms in spring are a joy to behold, especially where the plants have been allowed to form a carpet amongst established trees and shrubs. Plant single snowdrops, *Galanthus nivalis*, among the strawberry and this will provide early colour, the freshly emerging strawberry leaves hiding those of the snowdrop as they start to fade.

If you have a well-established hedge, then many of our popular hedgerow plants can be established along the base. If the hedge is only cut once a year, then allow old man's beard, *Clematis vitalba*, to scramble around, decorating it with starry white flowers and fluffy seed heads. Utilize the base for plants like red campion, *Silene dioica*, and ragged robin, *Lychnis flos cuculi*. Both are easily raised from seed and can be introduced as young plants, or else raised from seed sown on selected cleared sites at the base of the hedge. Foxgloves, *Digitalis purpurea*, are appropriate in such situations, along with perforate St. John's wort, *Hypericum perforatum*, and the common hedge parsley, *Torilis japonica*. None is likely to be invasive, but all add much to the informal garden scene.

If you have a wet patch of ground, establish a clump or two of the lovely fluffy white flowered meadowsweet, *Filipendula ulmaria*. This is grand during mid-summer when growing in a tangle of the azure-blue water forget-me-not, *Myosotis scorpioides*, or the pinkish-lilac water mint, *Mentha aquatica*. Marsh marigolds, *Caltha palustris*, can provide really early colour, flashing waxy golden blossoms amongst dark green scalloped foliage shortly after the last snow has departed. With the interesting, but unwieldy winter heliotrope, *Petasites grandiflorus*, the marsh marigolds are the earliest plants to enliven difficult damp spots after the dark and dreary days of winter.

A typical cottage garden can provide a home for many of our native plants, for it is here that they can be most readily integrated. The wild-flower boom in its present form is still something rather new and we have a lot to learn about the cultivation of plants in artificially created situations where the end result is intended to appear natural. I am not sure whether this is desirable in the cottage garden. Indeed, I am inclined to turn strongly against it. As I mentioned at the outset, cottage gardeners have always found space for desirable natives and I think that for now we should follow that tradition. Primroses struggling through a sward of coarse grass and fighting a battle with briars may be very natural, but I would prefer to see their pale yellow faces perfectly formed, peeping from amongst well grown leaves glistening with morning dew. If we are going to grow our native flora let us grow it well and enjoy it properly.

11

FLOWERS FOR WILDLIFE

Butterflies, bees and birds are as much a part of the cottage garden as the trees and flowers. In fact most gardens become wildlife refuges without any attention, but the wildlife which they contain varies and can be influenced considerably by the plant life which grows there. Simply exchanging one species for another can completely alter the ecology.

PLANTS FOR BIRD LIFE

Despite the popular assumption that gardeners dislike birds, it is a fact that most gardeners are bird lovers. It is true that they may not be enamoured by the attentions of wood pigeons or house sparrows, nor be particularly thrilled by the presence of a blackbird in the strawberry bed, but the others, apart from being decorative and lively, make some contribution towards controlling the pests that attack our garden plants.

The easiest and most successful plant to grow for the birds is the giant annual sunflower, *Helianthus annuus*. This is raised from seed sown directly in the open ground immediately after all danger of frost has passed. Provide a sheltered sunny situation, stake the plants as necessary and they will rapidly attain gigantic proportions. The enormous yellow flowers with dark brownish centres are loved by bees, a fact that did not go unnoticed by early gardeners who used to plant sunflowers amongst their runner beans in the hope of increasing the chances of pollination. However, it is the seeds for which the wildlife gardener grows them and which provide the birds with food and us with an acrobatic display. If the seeds are allowed to develop fully on the old flower head, members of the titmouse family will quickly discover them and perform all kind of antics in their effort to extract them from the hard green disc of the flower. Once the frost has blackened the old stalk and the seed head starts to sag, the seeds can be flicked out, dried, and fed to the birds in a conventional feeder.

Teasels attract not only blue tits, but more especially goldfinches. The common fullers teasel, *Dipsacus fullonum*, is a biennial and therefore seed needs sowing every year to ensure a continuity of plants. If sown in boxes during early summer, the neat rosettes of foliage are ready for transplanting during the early autumn. They need careful handling as they do not like root disturbance, so it is a good idea to raise young plants in individual plastic plant packs to ensure that they move with a proper rootball. As long as the soil is reasonably free draining, and they are not forced to endure the shade, then they are of very easy culture. Teasels are not spectacularly beautiful plants, but their flower heads have a distinct architectural quality which renders them suitable for general garden decoration. It is the seeds that the goldfinches go for, clinging to the spike heads and creating quite a stir. Apart from *Dipsacus fullonum*, there is the similar *D. sativus* and the more prickly *D. ferox*. Both are equally attractive to birds, but not perhaps so easy to place in the garden.

Berried trees and shrubs are beloved of birds, and while many of those already mentioned will provide winter food, there are several that never fail to attract attention. Of these the firethorns or pyracanthas are the most important. Capable of being grown as

A mixed border dominated by the lovely *Buddleia alternifolia* one of the
many late summer plants loved by butterflies.

free-standing shrubs, these versatile evergreens with thorned branches, creamy-white flowers and dense clusters of orange, red or yellow fruits, are more usually utilized as wall shrubs. There are many different kinds available from the nurseryman, but I have found that *Pyracantha coccinea* and its cultivar 'Lalandei' are most attractive to birds. If you want to grow a firethorn in order to enjoy the colourful fruits, then it is better to select *P. rogersiana*, or more especially its yellow berried cultivar 'Flava'. The birds tend to leave these two alone, the yellow berried form often retaining its fruits until late winter.

Cotoneasters are loved by birds, but it seems that *Cotoneaster salicifolius* and its various cultivars, especially the orange and red fruited ones are preferred. The common herringbone cotoneaster, *C. horizontalis* eventually loses its fruits, but those of *C. cornubia* last well into the new year without being bothered. No serious work seems to have been undertaken as to why one particular species or cultivar is preferred to another, but generally yellow and white fruited forms escape until all the orange and red berried kinds have been cleared up. So if birds are your passion, rather than berries, go for bright red fruited cultivars of species known to be vulnerable. If you want to know the most vulnerable kinds of any particular genus, consult your local nurseryman. He is bound to know, for he will have been pestered by customers requiring bird-proof varieties!

PLANTS FOR INSECT LIFE

Birds are not the only wildlife in the garden, butterflies are just as important. Plant some of the buddleias for them. Popularly known as butterfly bushes, these are amongst the most diverse and useful shrubs for the cottage garden, playing host to crowds of peacocks and tortoiseshells on warm summer days. *Buddleia davidii* is the type to plant, a quick growing medium sized shrub with dark green or glabrous, lanceolate leaves and fragrant, pale lilac or purple blossoms carried in graceful arching panicles. It is not particularly desirable in its original variable form, but the cultivars that it has sired are exceptional. 'Empire Blue' is the loveliest of all, a bold deep violet variety with conspicuous orange eyes and a stiff upright habit. For something a little darker the rather inappropriately named 'Black Knight' can be recommended. As with most plants that use the word black to describe them, this is really nothing more than deep purple, but nevertheless very desirable. 'Royal Red' does not really live up to its name either, for this has splendid wine coloured flowers rather than the red that one might expect. However, 'White Profusion' and 'White Bouquet' fulfil expectations, the latter having conspicuous yellow-eyed, flowers and creating a great white frothy fountain.

Buddleia davidii is unquestionably the most important species amongst the butterfly bushes, for it has been instrumental in providing a wealth of slightly off-beat, but colourful summer flowering shrubs. Not all are direct descendants from *B. davidii* for it is a promiscuous character and has united freely with other species to yield interesting and attractive progeny that are also desirable butterfly plants. The alleged union between *B. davidii* and *B. fallowiana* at Lochinch Gardens in Galloway has produced interesting results. Here both species hybridize freely and interesting forms have been selected, a particularly fine one with deep violet-mauve blossoms amongst grey-green, felty leaves being especially popular and now available under the name 'Lochinch'. A similar union has given rise to 'West Hill', a less desirable yet garden-worthy buddleia which resembles *B. fallowiana*, except for its immense panicles of lavender-blue flowers.

Buddleia alternifolia is a distinct species and clearly the odd man out, for it is the only buddleia with an alternate leaf arrangement. These clothe graceful arching stems which during mid-summer are transformed into cascades of soft purple by myriad intensely fragrant butterfly laden blossoms. These are borne on wood made the previous year, so customary spring pruning cannot be advocated, the mere thinning of branches after flowering being all that is necessary. If left to its own devices *B. alternifolia* makes a sizeable shrub of rather lax habit, so if you have limited space it is worth considering treating it as a half-standard.

The autumn flowering *Sedum spectabile* is another wonderful butterfly plant. This is that remarkable hardy, dwarf herbaceous perennial with light green, fleshy foliage reminiscent of a succulent, and large fluffy heads of deep rose-pink flowers. There are two good modern cultivars called 'Autumn Joy' and 'Meteor' which are more productive and weather resistant. Many autumn-flowering annual and perennial plants also attract butterflies, and in recent years I have been amazed to see how many different butterflies will alight on the semi-double blossoms of Coltness bedding dahlias. A little bright in colour, these can nevertheless be safely incorporated into the cottage garden. So can single French marigolds like 'Naughty Marietta'. Avoid the brassy fully double and crested modern kinds as these are totally out of keeping, even though they play host to butterflies in the same way as the single kinds.

Moths should not be overlooked, for although these are largely nocturnal, they do dance and play in the early evening, much to the gardener's enjoyment. Plant one of the older strains of flowering tobacco or nicotiana, such as 'Sensation', near your sitting out area; not only will you be delighted by their comings and goings, but entranced by the sweet fragrance of the tobacco flowers which heightens as darkness falls, in order to attract the moths. I have not yet observed the same activities with other hardy night fragrant plants like night scented stock, but careful observation would be well rewarded as most night scented flowers are pollinated by moths.

Bees go for most flowers, although some are great favourites. The majority of the plants considered under the chapter devoted to herbs and fragrant plants are good bee subjects, especially the tall blue borage, *Borago officinalis*, the common hyssop, *Hyssopus officinalis*, all the lavenders and the marjorams as well as the catmint, *Nepeta mussinii*. This latter is marvellous for bees and an extremely useful plant for edging paths. Beware though, for this fragrant grey-green leaved plant with its narrow spires of lilac-purple flowers can become so alive with bees that it is a hazardous business passing by.

We have had a cursory glance at some of the more prominent plants that attract wildlife, but we have barely touched upon the subject. What I hope to have done is to persuade you that a real cottage garden is not just a silent, colourful, fragrant picture, but a piece of paradise where birds and butterflies glide by and the air is filled with the hum of enterprising bees and passing insects. We have looked at the plants that we can deliberately plant to attract these creatures to our garden, but we have not investigated what we need to do in order to keep them there. Larval food plants, availability of water, nesting sites and much more form an integral part of the ecology of the garden. In the tangled informality of a cottage garden a natural balance is usually achieved without trying. With a little thought and effort it can be guaranteed.

12
NEW PLANTS FROM OLD

The propagation of your own plants is one of the most pleasurable and important activities to be undertaken in the establishment and maintenance of a cottage garden. Old plants require revitalizing periodically and new plants need raising regularly, especially annuals, biennials and short-lived herbaceous perennials. On economic grounds alone it makes sense to grow your own plants, but added enjoyment can be gained by swopping plants with fellow gardeners and propagating plants that are not widely commercially available. Propagation to the newcomer to gardening is something of a mystery and many old gardeners would like to keep it that way. Some forms of propagation, such as budding and grafting, are an art that it requires time to perfect, but the other methods are quite simple to master when you have an understanding of the plants' requirements.

HARDY ANNUALS FROM SEED

Hardy annuals can be sown during spring outside in the open ground in the positions in which they are to flower. However, having gardened from East Anglia northwards and regularly encountered the vagaries of our climate north of the home counties I would suggest that for most gardens a late spring sowing is more prudent, except on heavy clay soil in the north where an early summer sowing would be more acceptable. Little is gained by sowing seed early in cold uncompromising clay soil. Seeds sown under such conditions usually rot before they have had an opportunity to germinate. Use the calendar as a guide to sowing, but

be influenced more in your decisions by soil and weather conditions.

The success of hardy annuals sown directly outside owes as much to autumn soil preparation as to the skill of the gardener sowing the seed during the spring. A deeply cultivated soil with plenty of organic matter incorporated into it, and one that has been weathered over winter should be ideal. This will retain moisture during dry periods and if well weathered, will knock down with the hoe into a good friable medium that will be ready for seed sowing immediately. Indeed, the final preparation of soil that has been weathered should be left until just prior to sowing. Early tilth preparation will result in soil compaction if it rains before you have an opportunity to get the seeds in.

However, it is important that the soil is firm prior to sowing. Shuffle across the bed, drawing one foot up to the other as you go. One passage across the bed or border should be sufficient. After that create a shallow tilth with a rake. It is useful to apply any fertilizer at this stage. I prefer a simple balanced fertilizer like Growmore which comes in a granular form and can be distributed evenly over the surface of the soil prior to raking in. Always apply fertilizers to the manufacturer's instructions and never scatter them amongst seedlings and young plants or else severe leaf scorching will occur, especially if the weather is hot and dry.

When a border or bed is to be used exclusively for annuals, rather than the annuals merely used to fill in gaps in the mixed border, it is best to mark out the sites of individual varieties with a sprinkling of sand. Groups of an irregular shape and size always present the best visual effect. While taller varieties are usually better towards the back of the border, strict placement according to height is undesirable. The seeds of annuals are generally covered with about their own depth of soil, small seeds being carefully broadcast over their designated area and then raked in. The broadcasting of seed means the even distribution of seed by hand, using the eye as a judge as to the correct density and spread. Very fine seeds that are difficult to distribute evenly should be mixed with a little dry silver sand. This enables you to see the exact spread of the seed, assuming that the seed is equally distributed throughout the sand. Large seeds, like those of the nasturtium, require sowing individually in their final positions.

Newly sown seed and emerging seedlings must be carefully watched, especially during dry periods, and water must be given as necessary to ensure unchecked growth. Crowded seedlings should be thinned at the earliest opportunity if damping-off disease is to be avoided and strong healthy plants are to develop. Damping-off disease is characterized by black patches which appear at the base of the stems of seedlings at the point where they emerge from the soil. This basal rotting causes the seedlings to collapse.

Rarely are single plants affected, the disease being extremely virulent and causing considerable losses, especially during warm humid weather. Watering regularly with a product that has benomyl as the active ingredient will exercise some control. Alternatively the copper-based material, popularly referred to as Cheshunt compound can be used. This is available in a powdered form which is mixed with water and watered on to the seedlings every ten days or so. It is wise to use one of these materials as a preventative against damping off disease in any event.

Some annuals resent root disturbance, but many can be successfully moved in their seedling stage to another part of the garden. This is useful as it presents the opportunity of utilizing the seedlings thinned from main concentrations elsewhere. As most annual seedlings grow very quickly it is important to provide some kind of support early on. Brushwood is ideal and should be incorporated at the seedling stage in order to restrict root damage from the probing ends of the sticks. By staking early the young plants can grow through their twiggy support and disguise them quite naturally.

Seedling annuals are susceptible to slug damage, so it is prudent to scatter slug pellets amongst them at the same time as the stakes are being erected. Annuals of the Crucifer family, such as candytuft and Virginian stocks, are vulnerable to the attacks of flea beetles which make tiny holes in the seed leaves and turns them a pale sickly yellow-green, distorting the first true leaves as well. Attacks are most likely during dry weather, but a generous dusting with derris will help effect a control. To prevent a build-up of this pest in your garden, be sure to remove host weeds like charlock and shepherd's purse at the first opportunity.

RAISING HARDY BIENNIALS

Most of our spring flowering bedding subjects are hardy biennials, or else plants treated as such. There are two ways of raising these plants depending upon their mode of growth. Wallflowers and sweet williams are easiest raised in drills in the open ground, while forget-me-nots, pansies and polyanthus are best grown in trays or pots. All are sown during mid-summer in order to produce plants that are strong enough to be able to withstand the winter.

Plants that are best raised in the open garden are sown in shallow drills made with the edge of a swan-neck hoe in a nursery bed. This need not be a special part of the garden separated for the production of young plants, but can equally well be, and often is, a corner of the vegetable plot. If this is what you intend to do with wallflowers, be careful to include them in the section reserved for cabbages, cauliflowers and sprouts, for like brassicas, wallflower are subject to devastating attacks from club root disease and therefore could upset the rotation of your vegetable plot.

Before sowing, water the open drills and ensure that the soil is thoroughly moistened. The seed can then be distributed thinly along the bottom of the drill and back filled; if the weather is dry, water the drill again. Seedlings of wallflowers appear within a few days and so it is as well to be ready to dust them with derris dust as a precaution against flea beetle.

Once the first few adult leaves have appeared the vigorous young seedlings should be transplanted into nursery rows about 10 cm (4 in) apart with 25 cm (10 in) between the rows. As soon as these transplants have become established, the growing points should be pinched out so that they bush out and become more substantial plants. Within reason, the larger the plants, the fewer that will be required.

Open-ground plants can be moved to their final positions any time after the summer bedding has been cleared away. It is difficult to establish spring flowering bedding subjects after mid-autumn, so if the season lingers, the summer bedding must be removed and the soil prepared before then. Adequate soil preparation is vital for the success of these subjects, although fresh manure is not desirable. A slow release fertilizer (e.g. bonemeal) applied before planting, together with very firm planting will ensure the success of most spring flower subjects.

ANNUALS AND BEDDING PLANTS UNDER GLASS

Tender annuals and bedding plants can be raised from seed sown under glass or on the window ledge from mid-winter onwards, depending upon the varieties being grown and the conditions which you can provide. Some subjects need a long season of growth and these must be sown as early as possible. It is important though, that at the time of

sowing the ratio of light to heat is balanced, or else sickly seedlings will be produced. It is far more sensible to wait a couple of weeks if your conditions are not quite right before sowing, for although the resulting plants will not be as substantial, they will be much healthier and better balanced. Often the seeds of bedding plants are sown in the warmth of a living room or kitchen. The seedlings quickly germinate because of the warmth provided, but with the poor daylight that is inevitable so early in the year, they become drawn and leggy. The ratio of light and temperature is so out of balance that the young seedlings are not able to make satisfactory progress.

Even the gardener with a greenhouse can get caught out when making an early sowing. It is well known that most greenhouse owners over-estimate the temperature at which their greenhouse can be maintained. The sharp temperature drop associated with a spell of severe weather will have a marked effect upon seedlings, even if frost is kept at bay. Seedlings that receive such a check usually take a couple of weeks to recover and are then often distorted. In such circumstances you may just as well have left the sowing for a couple of weeks more and then had seedlings that would grow on vigorously and unchecked.

Seedlings being raised under glass should always be sown in trays or pans of good seed compost. Never be tempted to go out into the garden and scoop up some ordinary soil for seed raising. Unless your garden soil is exceptional, the physical structure will be poor and not conducive to the raising of many varieties, especially those with very fine seed. Garden soil will also be full of all kinds of pathogens which will almost inevitably cause problems later on. The seed that we purchase has the sole object in life of germinating, let us not hamper it with poor compost or growing conditions. Seed is an expensive commodity, so do not be tempted to skimp on the cost of a tray full of good compost. Remember that plants reflect directly the medium in which they are growing. It is important though, to carefully select the compost which you use. Seed composts, as opposed to potting composts, have few nutrients in them and are the ideal medium for seed germination and emergence. The lack of nutrients is deliberate and ensures that it is unlikely to damage tender seedlings, and that the growth of moss is as far as possible impaired.

Soil based composts, like the John Innes Seed Compost, are also suitable for bedding subjects, but quicker germination and initially better plants are produced from soil-less mediums. All peat, soil-less composts need treating with care and it is essential to be selective about what you sow in them.

Unless you can be sure of a very smooth surface once the seed tray is filled, it is unwise to sow fine seeded flowers like lobelia or petunia in the compost, as the material is fibrous and creates air pockets into which tiny seeds can become lost. All peat composts are first class for larger seeded plants like salvias and marigolds. Smaller seeded flowers can be sown in a soilless compost that also has a quantity of high quality sand mixed in with it. In any event, whatever your preference, go for a good branded sort. Unless you are going to use substantial amounts of seed compost I believe that it is both cheaper and safer to buy rather than to mix your own. Homemade compost can be very variable and the resulting plants unpredictable.

Procedure for sowing seed in trays

The pans or seed trays being used to raise seedlings should be filled with a suitable compost to within 1 cm ($\frac{3}{8}$ in) of the top (Fig. 12). A soil-based compost should be firmly tamped down before sowing, but a soilless kind merely needs putting in the pan or tray, filling to the rim and then tapping. Initial watering will settle it. Firming down soilless compost drives out the air and causes the formation of compact areas which seedling roots are unlikely to be able to ramify. It is useful though, with all kinds of

Fig 12. Seed sowing in trays.

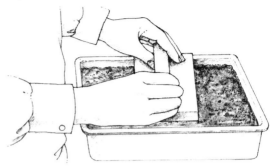

(a) When using a soil-based compost ensure that it is firm.

(b) Sprinkle seeds evenly over the surface.

(c) Cover the seeds lightly with sieved compost.

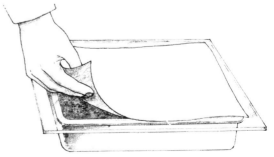

(d) Place a sheet of glass over the tray and cover with newspaper.

111

composts, to firm the corners and the edges with the fingers when filling a seed tray. This prevents sinking around the edges and the seed from being washed into the sides where it will germinate in a congested mass. Seed compost can be watered from above prior to sowing. This will settle the soilless type and allow for any deficiences caused by humps and hollows to be rectified.

Seeds of most annuals raised under glass are sprinkled thinly over the surface of the compost and then covered by about their own depth of the sowing medium. Large seeds can be sown individually at regular intervals so that the pricking out process is minimized. A light covering of compost then completes the operation. The covering of seeds with compost, except the tiniest ones and a few that require light to germinate, is a necessity but do not be tempted to over-do it.

Some seeds that we buy now are pelleted for easy handling and these require slightly different treatment. They should be sown in a moist friable compost and scarcely covered. It should not be so dry that the pellet will not break down, nor so wet that the pellet absorbs an excess of water and becomes a sticky mass enveloping and suffocating the seed. John Innes Seed Compost is ideal and, when moistened, can be said to be in a suitable condition if, when squeezed in the hand, it forms a lump which slowly falls apart. Pelleted seeds require the same temperature to germinate as ordinary seeds, but take a day or two longer to emerge.

Very fine seeds like petunia and lobelia are almost as fine as pepper and are very difficult to handle satisfactorily. Their distribution over the surface of the compost can be facilitated, however, by mixing a little dry silver sand in with the seed. This acts as a carrier and indicates the area of compost over which the seed has been distributed. Once fine seed has been sown it should be watered from beneath by standing the tray or pan in a bowl of water. Overhead watering is too hazardous and redistributes the seed unevenly.

Most seeds benefit from bottom heat, so when a heating cable is available full use should be made of this facility. Warm compost promotes rapid germination in the majority of annual flowers. Indeed, in an unheated greenhouse the combination of a soil warming cable and a sheet of glass placed over the seed tray can create a remarkably effective microclimate. Additionally, a sheet of newspaper placed over the glass will act as extra insulation and still permit sufficient light to pass through until the seedlings are fully germinated. Both glass and paper should be removed immediately emergence is complete.

As soon as the seedlings have appeared they should be placed in a position in which they can receive maximum light to ensure that they develop into stocky, short-jointed plants. At this stage damping-off disease can once again be a problem and either benomyl or Cheshunt compound must be resorted to.

Pricking out

Seedlings should be pricked out as soon as they are large enough to handle. This means that the individual seedlings are lifted from the clusters in which they germinated and spaced out into a pan or seed tray (Fig. 13). Standard seed trays will comfortably accommodate thirty-five plants, although with smaller growing subjects as many as forty-five seedlings can be grown. Ideally seedlings should have their seed or cotyledon leaves fully expanded before transplanting and the first true leaf showing. Care must be taken in handling the seedlings as they are very delicate and often brittle. Never hold a seedling by its root or stem, always by the tip of a seed leaf. Rough handling at the pricking-out stage can quite easily lead to the spread of the damping-off disease, the pathogen attacking damaged stem tissue. It is usual to prick out seedlings slightly lower in the compost than in the tray or pan in which they germinated, in most cases burying the stem up to the level of the seed leaves. This only applies if the seedlings are short, strong and healthy. Burying a lanky

Fig 13. Pricking out.

(*a*) Seedlings should be lifted as soon as large enough to handle.

(*b*) Space them out evenly in seed trays using potting compost.

seedling will result in its collapse.

It is usual to prick seedlings out into potting compost rather than seed compost as they are going to require considerable nourishment. Any standard soil-less potting compost should serve, although feeding with a liquid manure may be necessary later on. John Innes No 1 is the most satisfactory soil based compost to use, although the seedlings will also need regular feeding a

month or so before the plants are put out in the garden. Provided that there are not severe temperature fluctuations and always plenty of light, the plants should grow on well. Apart from perhaps mildew and greenfly, few problems are likely to be encountered in the well-organized greenhouse. Both of these hazards can be easily countered with any of the popular systemic fungicides or insecticides currently available. The most critical time in the raising of half-hardy bedding subjects is the weaning period, when the plants are eased out of their comfortable greenhouse or kitchen windowsill atmosphere and placed in a frame prior to planting in the open garden.

A cold frame is ideal for this, for in cold weather the frame light can remain in place, whereas if the weather turns warmer it can be removed entirely. What must be achieved is a gradual tolerance of lower temperatures over a period of two or three weeks without giving the plants a check. First of all the frame light is lifted to permit ventilation. This is gradually increased until the frame light can be removed entirely during the daytime. It can then be raised at night to allow ventilation, except when a frost threatens. Eventually the light can be removed both day and night unless frost or heavy rain threatens.

When a frame is not available, a similar effect can be provided by taking the plants outside during the day and standing them in a sheltered place, returning them indoors at night. The weaning process can continue until the plants take on a hardy appearance. This is typified by a stiffness of foliage, usually associated with a darker green colour. A bluish-green colour indicates a check caused through chilling and the plants will often take several weeks to recover.

HARDY PERENNIALS FROM SEED

Seed raising of herbaceous perennials has its limitations, for few of the best-named herbaceous plants come absolutely true from seed. *Geum* 'Mrs. Bradshaw' is one that does, but the majority are mixed strains. That is not to say that there is anything wrong with a mixture, for one of the finest seed raised perennials is the Russell lupin, seen at its best in a reselected seed-raised strain. However, it is for the species like *Lychnis chalcedonica* and *Physalis alkekengii* that most gardeners consider seed raising.

Traditionally sown during early summer, perennials like this produce a flowering-size plant the following year. There is no reason why earlier sowings cannot be made, it is just that these usually conflict with the spring rush in the garden. Perennials with fine seed are best started in a good seed compost in a seed tray and raised with the protection of a cold frame, but larger seeded kinds and those with high germination rates can be raised in a nursery bed alongside the wallflowers and sweet williams. If it is possible, the best plants are obtained by raising the seedlings in trays and then potting the individual plants into peat or fibre pots and growing them on in a frame.

While most perennials which are raised from seed require warm equitable conditions in which to germinate freely, a number require chilling in order to break their dormancy. What happens in nature is that if conditions for germination are not amenable when the seed matures and falls to the ground, an embryo inhibitor acts to render the seed dormant until it has experienced a winter. It is the onset of frost during winter that effectively sends a message to the embryo which releases it from its dormancy.

Most gardeners are quite naturally reluctant to freeze seeds, but if sown in the normal way and the pans placed in a freezer for a week or ten days, subsequently to be removed to a warm light environment, germination will quickly follow. Once the reason for this seemingly barbaric treatment of tiny seeds is appreciated, gardeners will usually shed any reluctance to deep freeze seeds.

TREES AND SHRUBS FROM SEED

We are not going to discuss here the raising of trees and shrubs like *Laburnum* and *Cytisus* which germinate freely if treated as ordinary herbaceous perennials. My concern here is for those specialized groups which are so important in the cottage garden scene, but do not fall into any of the categories hitherto mentioned. I am thinking now of, for example, the seeds of berried trees and shrubs. These usually come to hand in the remnants of the fruit and in most cases it is impossible to separate the seeds from the shrivelled flesh. If sown intact in a very sandy medium and exposed to the winter weather, or given the deep freezing treatment, they will germinate quite freely. When stood outside, the seed trays should be protected from birds.

Most conifers also germinate freely if exposed to the elements, and although they can be successfully raised in John Innes Seed Compost, subsequent growth is much enhanced by the use of forest litter. This is in effect the sweepings of pine or spruce needles gathered from beneath mature trees, mixed with some of the top layer of soil. It is not a very pleasant medium to look at, but it does contain the very important mycorrhiza or soil fungi which associate with this group of plants and results in stronger seedlings of speedier growth.

EVERGREENS FROM CUTTINGS

Both broad-leaved evergreens and conifers can be propagated from cuttings taken either during early autumn or late spring. That is all except the needle-bearing conifers like *Picea*, *Abies* and *Pinus*. There are admittedly exceptions, but these are few and far between. Cuttings of any kind of plant have the advantage of reproducing that individual and are the main way of increasing named cultivars of garden plants. It must also be said that the resulting plant will depend to a great extent upon the material from which the cutting was taken. Therefore a cutting removed from an upright conifer that was growing in a prostrate or pendent manner will not necessarily yield an upright plant, even though genetically the plant will be the same. Similarly a prostrate conifer that throws up occasional erect shoots cannot be guaranteed to remain prostrate in its progeny if cutting material is taken from that upright shoot. So careful selection with evergreens, especially conifers, is vital if the resulting plants are going to be of the desired form.

Cuttings should be selected from branches that are not too old and woody, nor too soft and immature. Take pieces of shoot up to 10 cm (4 in) long and pull them away from the older wood so that a heel or piece of older wood remains attached to the base of each cutting. This ensures a good chance of rooting. Immature wood of the previous season's growth is always difficult to encourage to root. Place the cuttings in a cold frame or sheltered position in the garden in trays of compost consisting of equal parts sedge peat and sharp sand.

Before each cutting is inserted dip the raw end in a hormone-rooting powder. This not only activates the cells on the cut surface to produce roots, but containing a fungicide helps to prevent the cuttings from rotting off in cool damp conditions. Some cuttings will root very quickly, amongst them the cherry laurel, *Prunus laurocerasus*, but others will take several months. While cool damp conditions will cause problems with rotting, the cuttings must never be allowed to dry out completely and will require occasional watering and spraying overhead.

SHRUBS FROM HARDWOOD CUTTINGS

Hardwood cuttings are pieces of mature wood from the previous season's growth which have firm, hardened tissue. They are removed from the parent plant after leaf fall, often being derived directly from prunings made at that time. A wide range of shrubs can be propagated in this manner and despite the fact that for many subjects it is considered to be an old-fashioned and outmoded technique, it is the easiest way for a gardener without any propagation facilities to increase many of the decorative shrubs in his garden.

It is best to select hardwood cuttings from vegetative rather than flowering wood, taking care not to use thin pieces that are likely to become desiccated before rooting, nor stems that are thicker than a pencil, for these will be too old to root readily. Wood should be of solid cross-section. Hollow cuttings are most unlikely to root satisfactorily. Ideal material is usually of a light brown colour, full of the vigour of youth and about 20 cm (8 in) long.

If the shrub is intended to have a leading growth, then the material should be selected from terminal shoots, but if it is intended to be bushy and break from low down, then there is no reason why a length of stem cannot be cut into two or three pieces without worrying about a terminal bud. Cuttings should always be removed at a leaf joint as this is the area where the root-forming cambium cells are more numerous. If the cut is made at an angle through the leaf joint the maximum area of these cells will be exposed.

Specific rooting powders are available for the treatment of hardwood cuttings, but nowadays general hormone-rooting powders fulfil this role. The end of each cutting is dipped into the powder and the surplus knocked off before planting. This stimulates rooting and once again there is the value of the fungicide which helps prevent rotting before rooting. While the chances of rooting are enhanced by the use of a specially prepared medium, most common flowering shrubs can be rooted directly outside in the open ground.

It is important that the soil is in good condition and that the cut surface of the cutting makes firm contact with it. The cutting is usually pushed into the soil for about half its length, but before doing this you should decide whether the resulting shrub is intended to branch from the base or yield a shrub on a short stem. If a shrub that is well branched from the base is required, then leave all the buds on the cutting when it is inserted. If a short clear stem is wanted, then all the lower buds must be removed to prevent suckering.

Most gardeners insert hardwood cuttings in neat rows in the open ground with 5–6 cm (2–2½ in) between each cutting. Commercially, cuttings are bundled in 25s or 50s, tied together with string or raffia and inserted into the soil in a bunch. Either way they seem to root well, so it depends upon the quantity that you are taking and the time at your disposal as to which method you choose. On heavy land it is useful to sprinkle a little sharp sand into the trench to allow free drainage.

When cuttings are going to be rooted under more controlled conditions in a selected medium in a frame, then they should be accommodated in deep plant pots. A mixture of equal parts sharp sand and sedge peat, or peat and perlite provides an excellent rooting medium. However, when rooting such cuttings in a frame be careful not to promote unnatural soft growth. Leaving the frame lights off in all but the harshest weather will ensure good hardy plants. From either frame or open ground, rooted cuttings will be ready for potting or lining out in a nursery bed from late spring.

SOFTWOOD CUTTINGS OF SHRUBS AND PERENNIALS

Many decorative shrubs can be increased from cuttings of semi-ripe wood taken during late summer. Soft unripe wood can be utilized earlier, but unless you can provide conditions of warmth and high humidity, together with plenty of attention, then re-sults are going to be variable. I much prefer taking cuttings from the so-called semi-ripe shoots which are still healthy and green, but are just taking on a purplish caste. The stems are soft and supple, but not so soft that they wilt almost immediately after cutting. The most satisfactory cuttings are made from short pieces of healthy, unflowered stem cut at a leaf joint. Once again this is important as it is here that the greatest cellular activity takes place.

Remove the lower leaves of each cutting and any others that are likely to rest upon the rooting medium and decompose. Large upper leaves can also be reduced in number by the judicious use of the knife and this will further reduce moisture loss through transpiration. Provide a rooting medium of equal parts sedge peat and sharp sand or peat and perlite and rooting will be fairly rapid. Once this is known to have taken place, pot each cutting individually and gradually harden it off, treating it as a pot plant until the following year.

Stem cuttings of many herbaceous plants can be taken in early spring just as the shoots are appearing through the soil. Lupins and delphiniums are excellent examples of plants which can be increased this way. Shoots no more than 10 cm (4 in) long should be removed with a sharp knife at a leaft joint and rooted in a standard rooting medium in a cold frame. Ensure that the stem of each cutting is solid. Hollow-stemmed cuttings will not root and should be discarded. It is useful to use a hormone-rooting powder on the cut surface as this not only assists in root initiation but also, by virtue of the fungicidal content, helps prevent the cuttings from rotting. If close conditions are maintained rooting should be rapid and the cuttings can be transferred to individual pots prior to weaning.

ROOT CUTTINGS

Root cuttings can be taken from many herbaceous plants and are one of the simplest methods of increasing those like the oriental poppy and others that do not divide properly or come true from seed. Cuttings are taken during the dormant period, the adult plant being lifted and the roots exposed. Suitable cutting material is then removed and the parent plant replanted without any harm having been done to it. The best material for rooting will be found on roots that are full of the vigour of youth. They should be substantial enough to be able to survive without desiccating and yet ideally should be no thicker than a pencil.

They should be cut into sections about 3 cm (1¼ in) long, laid horizontally in trays of a compost consisting of equal parts by volume of peat and sharp sand, and then lightly covered and watered and placed in a cold frame. Young plants should result by the following spring. The best time to take root cuttings is mid to late autumn as the plants produced will then be ready for potting up during early spring.

PROPAGATING BULBS AND CORMS

While few gardeners ever think of propagating their own bulbs, there is no reason why they should not, for the keen cottage gardener will doubtless acquire some old and perhaps not commercially available varieties which can only be distributed and preserved by the efforts of those gardeners growing them. Nothing complicated need be undertaken, for many bulbs like narcissus produce young bulblets. These cluster around the parents and periodically need lifting and dividing. For those that do not lend themselves to this method of reproduction there are a number of techniques available that deserve closer observation.

Most bulbs, when well established, benefit from being lifted and replanted every four or five years, daughter bulbs being removed and transplanted separately either in a nursery bed or elsewhere in the garden. If left in a congested mass they deteriorate anyway. It is vital with all young bulbs that they have an independent basal plate from which roots can grow. Small bulbs torn away from the parent have little chance of survival and leave the mature bulb open to fungal infection. Tulips have bulbs which are replaced after flowering by one or several new bulbs. On heavy land, or where summer bedding is to follow, gardeners often lift their tulips. It is at this time that daughter bulbs can be removed and placed in a nursery bed. Drying young bulbs off does no harm and planting can take place in the early autumn.

Corms, like those of crocus and gladioli, replace themselves each year. While spawn or tiny cormlets often cluster around the adults and can be removed for replanting, it is just a means of helping young plantlets on their way rather than strictly practical propagation such as has to be applied to hyacinths. While a few progeny will often group around the main bulb, it is largely a matter of chance.

To ensure a prolific crop of bulbils it is essential to damage the base plate. A healthy mature bulb is inverted and the conspicuous circular area beneath called the base plate is slashed with a knife. Usually two slivers of tissue are removed at right angles, thereby forming a cross. It is along the line of these incisions that the bulbils will cluster. It is important when cutting the base plate that none of the soft tissue of the bulb is damaged as this provides access for fungal diseases. The slashed bulb can be planted in the normal fashion in the open ground or else potted or boxed in a good friable compost; the latter method will yield the best results. Within a few months masses of young bulbs will have gathered around the incisions and these can be removed and planted in seed trays like little seeds. The bulbs will take up to four years or so to attain flowering size.

As mentioned in Chapter 8, many lilies, especially those derived from *Lilium tigrinum* and its allies can be increased from the tiny bulbils which gather in the axils of the main flowering stems. Others that cannot be increased this way can be reproduced by scaling. This involves the removal of healthy bulb scales from mature lily bulbs and inserting them in a peaty compost. Scales are carefully removed from the base plate of the bulb during the dormant period, ensuring that they come away clean and are not merely snapped off.

They are inserted more or less upright in the compost, but are covered with the medium. By mid-summer leaves will have been produced from them and the little plantlets can be potted up individually. From these little plants new bulbs will develop which will be of flowering size in three or five years depending upon the variety. It is necessary with lilies grown from scales to give a little protection. Some gardeners like to raise bulbils with heat, but a cold frame is perfectly adequate until the bulbs are large enough to plant out.

RAISING FERNS FROM SPORES

Growing ferns from spores is not a difficult proposition, but a useful one for the cottage gardener as many of the lovely hardy ferns which can be utilized in the garden are readily increased this way. Providing that you realize that the fern spores are not the flowering plant's exact equivalent of seed and therefore require slightly different treatment to conventional seeds, then you are unlikely to encounter any problem. In fact you might say that the spores of a fern are more or less equivalent to the pollen of a flowering plant. While spores can be purchased from the seedsman, the degree of success achieved is variable so it is better to gather fresh spores wherever possible.

With most ferns these are borne on the undersides of the fronds, although occasionally they occur in dense plume-like terminal clusters from the centre of the plant. When ripe the spores are cast on to the wind and it is at this time that they should be collected. The easiest method is to enclose the fertile frond in a large paper bag, breaking off the frond stalk and upturning both the frond and the bag. Given a vigorous shaking, the spores will detach themselves and fall to the bottom of the bag.

The spores of most species benefit from being sown immediately after collection, especially those from the royal fern, *Osmunda regalis*, as they contain a small amount of highly perishable chlorophyll which renders them viable for just a few days. Raising the spores need not be complicated and the method that I use has been successful for the majority of the hardy kinds likely to be attempted.

Sterilized clay pans are filled with a compost comprising, by volume, three parts peat, one part loam and a dusting of crushed charcoal to keep the mixture sweet. The whole surface area of the pan is then covered with a layer of finely crushed brick dust and the spores sown on this in the same way as one might sow fine seed like that of lobelia or begonia. A small square of glass is then placed over the top of the pan which is stood in a saucer of water in a warm, partially shaded position.

It depends upon the species or variety being grown, but about three weeks after sowing a green mossy growth will begin to smother the surface of the pan. This consists of thousands of little scale-like growths called prothalli which have both male and female elements. Under close humid conditions these elements unite to form embryos, which in turn germinate and produce young fern plants. As soon as the first fronds of these tiny ferns are recognizable the glass should be removed to allow for the free passage of air and to reduce the incidence of damping-off disease. When the young plantlets are large enough to handle they can be lifted in little clumps, the individual baby ferns teased out, and then planted in trays of compost in the same way as you might deal with ordinary bedding plants.

APPENDIX

The following tables list the principal plants included in the text and their main characteristics. Heights and spreads generally refer to those species and cultivars cited in the text.

1. Hedging
2. Broad-leaved evergreen shrubs
3. Conifers
4. Flowering shrubs
5. Decorative trees
6. Climbing and scrambling plants
7. Annual flowers
8. Biennial flowers
9. Hardy herbaceous perennials
10. Hardy ferns
11. Hardy ornamental grasses
12. Spring-flowering bulbs, corms and tubers
13. Summer-flowering bulbs
14. Herbs and fragrant plants
15. Wild flowers
16. Plants for wildlife

Readers are requested to note that the plants in each table are listed according to alphabetical order of Latin names; where applicable the common name is also given.

Abbreviations

cm = centimetre(s)
e. = early
fol. = foliage
fr. = fruit(s)
ft = foot/feet
inf. = informal
l. = late
m = metre(s)
vari. = variegated

1. HEDGING

Name	Flower/foliage	Season	Habit
Berberis	yellow flowers/evergreen	summer	inf.
Buxus Box	green/vari./evergreen	all year	formal
Cotoneaster	white flowers red/orange fruits/semi-evergreen	spring/autumn	inf.
Escallonia	white/pink/red flowers/evergreen	summer	formal/inf.
Forsythia	yellow/deciduous	spring	inf.
Ilex Holly	green/vari./evergreen	all year	formal
Lavandula Lavender	blue/purple/semi-evergreen	summer	inf.
Ligustrum Privet	green/vari. evergreen	all year	formal
Olearia	white/evergreen	summer	inf.
Prunus	white/pink deciduous	spring	formal
Rosmarinus Rosemary	blue/semi-evergreen	summer	formal/inf.
Santolina Cotton lavender	grey/green semi-evergreen	all year	inf.

2. BROAD-LEAVED EVERGREEN SHRUBS

Name	*Flower/foliage*	*Season*	*Height*	*Spread*
Elaeagnus	grey/green/vari. fol.	all year	1.2–3 m (4–10 ft)	1.2–2 m (4–6½ ft)
Garrya	greyish green catkins	winter	1.2–3 m (4–10 ft)	1.2–2 m (4–6½ ft)
Ilex Holly	green/vari.	all year	1.5–10 m (5–33 ft)	1.5–3 m (5–10 ft)

3. CONIFERS

Name	*Foliage*	*Height*	*Spread*
Abies Fir	green/blue-grey	1.2–30 m (4–100 ft)	1.5–3 m (5–10 ft)
Chamaecyparis Cypress	green/gold/blue	1–10 m (3¼–33 ft)	1–1.5 m (3¼–5 ft)
Thuja Arbor vitae	green/gold	1–10 m (3¼–33 ft)	1–1.5 m (3¼–5 ft)

4. FLOWERING SHRUBS

Name	*Flower/foliage*	*Season*	*Height*	*Spread*
Corylus Hazelnut	yellow catkins	e. spring	1–2 m (3¼–6½ ft)	1–1.5 m (3¼–5 ft)
Cydonia Japanese quince	white/orange/red	spring	1–2 m (3¼–6½ ft)	1–1.5 m (3¼–5 ft)
Cytisus Broom	white/yellow/purple	e. summer	60 cm–2 m (2–6½ ft)	30 cm–1.5 m (1–5 ft)
Daphne	white/purple	spring	90 cm–1.8 m (3–6 ft)	90 cm–1 m (3–3¼ ft)
Forsythia	yellow	spring	60 cm–2 m (2–6½ ft)	60 cm–1.5 m (2–5 ft)
Genista Broom	yellow	e. summer	30 cm–2 m (1–6½ ft)	30 cm–1.5 m (1–5 ft)
Hypericum	yellow	summer	30 cm–1.2 m (1–4 ft)	30–60 cm (1–2 ft)
Potentilla	white/yellow/pink	summer	30–90 cm (1–3 ft)	30–90 cm (1–3 ft)
Rhododendron	white/red/pink/purple	e. summer	30 cm–1.8 m (1–6 ft)	30 cm–1.5 m (1–5 ft)
Ribes Currants	red/pink	spring	1–2 m (3½–6½ ft)	1–1.5 m (3¼–5 ft)
Rosa Rose hybrid tea	white/pink/red/yellow	summer	60 cm–1 m (1–3¼ ft)	45–60 cm (1½–2 ft)
Rosa Rose floribunda	white/pink/red/yellow	summer	60 cm–1.5 m (1–5 ft)	45–90 cm (1½–3 ft)
Rubus Brambles	white/pink also coloured stems	summer winter	1.5–2 m (5–6½ ft)	1–1.5 cm (3¼–5 ft)
Syringa Lilac	white/pink/lilac	e. summer	1.5–3 m (5–10 ft)	1.5–2 m (5–6½ ft)
Viburnum	white/pink	winter	1.5–3 m (5–10 ft)	1.5–2 m (5–6½ ft)
Vinca Periwinkle	white/blue/purple	summer	30–60 cm (1–2 ft)	30–60 cm (2–3 ft)

5. DECORATIVE TREES

Name	*Flower/foliage*	*Season*	*Height*	*Spread*
Acer Maple	green/gold/purple fol.	summer/ autumn	1.5–10 m (5–33 ft)	1.5–4 m (5–13 ft)
Malus Crab apple	white/pink/autumn fruits	e. summer	2–10 m (6½–33 ft)	2–4 m (6½–13 ft)

Decorative Trees *contd.*

Name	Flower/foliage	Season	Height	Spread
Mespilus Medlar	white/autumn fruits	spring	2–10 m (6½–33 ft)	2–4 m (6½–13 ft)
Prunus Cherry, Apricot, Peach	white/pink/autumn fruits	spring	2–10 m (6½–33 ft)	2–4 m (6½–13 ft)
Pyrus Pear	white	spring	1.5–3 m (5–10 ft)	1.5–3 m (5–10 ft)
Rhus Sumach	red/orange fol.	autumn	1.5–3 m (5–10 ft)	1.5–3 m (5–10 ft)
Sambucus Elderberry	white/gold or green fol.	spring	1.5–3 m (5–10 ft)	1.5–3 m (5–10 ft)
Sorbus aria White beam	white/red or orange fruits	summer	2–10 m (6½-33 ft)	2–4 m (6½–13 ft)
Sorbus aucuparia Rowan	white/red or orange fruits	summer	2–10 m (6½–33 ft)	2–4 m (6½–13 ft)

6. CLIMBING AND SCRAMBLING PLANTS

Name	Flower/foliage	Season
Campsis	orange/red/yellow	summer
Clematis	white/purple/yellow red/pink	spring/ summer
Hedera Ivy	green/green and cream variegated foliage	all year round
Hydrangea	white/blue	summer
Lonicera Honeysuckle	white/yellow/purple	summer
Parthenocissus Virginia creeper	orange-red foliage	autumn
Passiflora Passion flower	blue and white	summer
Polygonum	white	l. summer
Rosa Roses	white/red/pink/yellow	summer
Wisteria	lavender-blue/white	summer

7. ANNUAL FLOWERS

Name	Flower colour	Season	Height	Spread
Antirrhinum Snap-dragon	most colours	summer	15–60 cm (6 in–2 ft)	15–30 cm (6 in–1 ft)
Calendula Pot marigold	yellow/orange	summer	15–60 cm (6 in–2 ft)	15–30 cm (6 in–1 ft)
Callistephus Aster	pink/red/blue/white	summer	30–60 cm (1–2 ft)	30–40 cm (1–1 ft 4 in)
Centaurea; Cornflower, Sweet sultan	blue/white/pink	summer	30–60 cm (1–2 ft)	20–30 cm (8 in–1 ft)

Annual Flowers *contd*.

Name	Flower colour	Season	Height	Spread
Clarkia	pink/red/white	summer	30–60 cm (1–2 ft)	20–30 cm (8 in–1 ft)
Cosmos	pink/red/yellow/white	summer	30–75 cm (1–2½ ft)	30–40 cm (1–1 ft 4 in)
Delphinium Larkspur	pink/blue/white	summer	60–90 cm (1–3 ft)	30–40 cm (1–1 ft 4 in)
Dianthus Pinks and Carnations	pink/red/white	summer	30–60 cm (1–2 ft)	30–40 cm (1–1 ft 4 in)
Iberis Candytuft	red/pink/white	summer	15–30 cm (6 in–1 ft)	15–20 cm (6–8 in)
Lathyrus Sweet peas	blue/white/red	summer	climbing	
Lavatera Mallow	pink/white	summer	60–90 cm (1–3 ft)	30–45 cm (1–1½ ft)
Limnanthes Poached egg plant	white and yellow	summer	15 cm (6 in)	15 cm (6 in)
Nigella Love-in-a-mist	blue/white	summer	45–60 cm (1½–2 ft)	30 cm (1 ft)
Verbena	red/white/purple	summer	15–45 cm (6 in–1½ ft)	15–30 cm (6 in–1 ft)

8. BIENNIAL FLOWERS

Name	Flower colour	Season	Height	Spread
Bellis Daisy	pink/red/white	spring	15–23 cm (6–9 in)	15 cm (6 in)
Cheiranthus Wallflowers	red/yellow/orange/white	spring	30–45 cm (1–1½ ft)	20–30 cm (8 in–1 ft)
Dianthus Sweet William	red/pink/white	spring/ e. summer	30–60 cm (1–2 ft)	30 cm (1 ft)
Myosotis Forget-me-nots	blue/white	spring	15–30 cm (6 in–1 ft)	15–20 cm (6–8 in)
Primula Polyanthus	red/pink/white/blue	spring	30 cm (1 ft)	15–30 cm (6 in–1 ft)
Viola Pansy	red/blue/white	spring/ e. summer	15–23 cm (6–9 in)	15–20 cm (6–8 in)

9. HARDY HERBACEOUS PERENNIALS

Name	Flower/foliage	Season	Height	Spread
Alstroemeria Peruvian lilies	pink/orange	summer	90 cm–1.2 m (3–4 ft)	90 cm (3 ft)
Aster Michaelmas daisies	white/pink/blue	autumn	23 cm–1.5 m (9 in–5 ft)	30–90 cm (1–3 ft)
Campanula Bellflowers	white/blue	spring/ summer	15 cm–1.2 m (6 in–4 ft)	15–90 cm (6 in–3 ft)
Chrysanthemum Shasta daisies	white	summer	30–90 cm (2–3 ft)	30–90 cm (1–3 ft)
Convallaria Lily of the valley	white/pink	e. summer	15–30 cm (6 in–1 ft)	15 cm + (6 in +)
Delphinium	white/blue/pink	summer	60 cm–1.8 m (2–6 ft)	30–90 cm (1–3 ft)

Hardy Herbaceous Perennials *contd.*

Name	Flower/foliage	Season	Height	Spread
Dianthus Pinks and Carnations	white/pink/red	summer	15–45 cm (6 in–1½ ft)	30 cm (1 ft)
Digitalis Foxgloves	white/pink/yellow	summer	30 cm–1.5 m (1–5 ft)	30–60 cm (1–2 ft)
Helleborus Christmas and Lenten roses	white/pink	winter/ spring	23–45 cm (9 in–1½ ft)	30 cm (1 ft)
Hemerocallis Daylilies	yellow/orange	summer	30–90 cm (1–3 ft)	30–45 cm (1–1½ ft)
Hosta Plantain lilies	green/blue/ variegated fol.	spring/ summer	15–45 cm (6 in–1½ ft)	30–45 cm (1–1½ ft)
Iris	white/orange/ yellow/blue pink	summer	30–1.2 cm (1–4 ft)	23–30 cm (9 in–1 ft)
Lupinus Lupins	white/blue/pink/ yellow/red	summer	60 cm–1.2 m (2–4 ft)	30–45 cm (1–1½ ft)
Mimulus Musk	red/yellow/orange	summer	10–45 cm (4 in–1½ ft)	23–30 cm (9 in–1 ft)
Oenothera Evening primroses	yellow	summer	30–90 cm (1–3 ft)	30–45 cm (1–1½ ft)
Papaver Poppies	white/pink/ orange/red	summer	30 cm–1.2 m (1–4 ft)	30–45 cm (1–1½ ft)
Phlox	white/pink/red/ lavender	l. summer	60 cm–1.2 m (2–4 ft)	30–45 cm (1–1½ ft)
Polygonatum Solomon's seal	white	summer	60–90 cm (2–3 ft)	30–45 cm (1–1½ ft)
Pyrethrum	white/pink/red	summer	30–60 cm (1–2 ft)	30–45 cm (1–1½ ft)
Scabious	blue	summer	60–90 cm (1–3 ft)	30–45 cm (1–1½ ft)
Smilacina False Solomon's Seal	white	summer	60–75 cm (1–1½ ft)	30–45 cm (1–1½ ft)
Viola Violets	purple/white	spring/ summer	15–30 cm (6 in–1 ft)	15–30 cm (6 in–1 ft)

10. HARDY FERNS

Name	Foliage	Season	Height	Spread
Asplenium Spleen-worts, Hart's tongue	green	all year	15–60 cm (6 in–2 ft)	15–60 cm (6 in–2 ft)
Athyrium Lady fern	green	summer	30–90 cm (1–3 ft)	30 cm (1 ft)
Blechnum Hard fern	green	all year	30–60 cm (1–2 ft)	30 cm (1 ft)
Dryopteris Male fern	green	summer	30 cm–1.2 m (1–4 ft)	30–45 cm (1–1½ ft)
Matteucia Ostrich feather fern	green	summer	60–90 cm (2–3 ft)	30–45 cm (1–1½ ft)
Onoclea Sensitive fern	green	summer	30–60 cm (1–2 ft)	30 cm (1 ft)
Polypodium Polypodys	green	all year	30–45 cm (1–1½ ft)	30 cm (1 ft)
Polystichum Shield fern	green	summer/ autumn	30–90 cm (1–3 ft)	15–45 cm (6–1½ ft)

11. HARDY ORNAMENTAL GRASSES

Name	Flower/foliage	Season	Height	Spread
Briza Quaking grass	fawn	summer	30–45 cm (1–1½ ft)	30 cm (1 ft)
Elymus Lyme grass	blue fol.	summer	30–60 cm (1–2 ft)	30 cm + (1 ft +)
Festuca Fescue	blue/green fol.	summer	15–30 cm (6 in–1 ft)	15–30 cm (6 in–1 ft)
Glyceria Manna grass	green/cream vari. fol.	summer	30–90 cm (1–3 ft)	30–60 cm (1–2 ft)
Hordeum Squirrel-tail grass	fawn	summer	30–75 cm (1–2½ ft)	30 cm (1 ft)
Lagurus Hare's tail	fawn	summer	30–75 cm (1–2½ ft)	30 cm (1 ft)
Miscanthus Hardy sugar cane	green/ vari. fol.	summer	60 cm–1.8 m (2–6 ft)	60–75 cm (2–2½ ft)
Phalaris Gardeners' garters	cream/green vari. fol.	summer	60–90 cm (2–3 ft)	30 cm (1 ft)
Polypogon Beard grass	fawn	summer	30–45 cm (6 in–1½ ft)	30 cm (1 ft)
Setaria Bristle grass	fawn	summer	30–90 cm (1–3 ft)	30 cm (1 ft)
Stipa Feather grass	fawn	summer	45–90 cm (1½–3 ft)	30 cm (1 ft)
Zea Maize	green/ vari. fol.	summer	60 cm–1.2 m (2–4 ft)	30 cm (1 ft)

12. SPRING FLOWERING BULBS, CORMS AND TUBERS

Name	Flower	Height
Chionodoxa Glory of the snow	blue and white	15 cm (1 ft)
Crocus	white/purple/yellow	up to 15 cm (1 ft)
Cyclamen	red/pink/white	10–15 cm (4–6 in)
Eranthis Winter aconite	yellow	10–15 cm (4–6 in)
Galanthus Snowdrop	white	10–15 cm (4–6 in)
Hyacinthus Hyacinth	blue/white/pink	20–30 cm (8 in–1 ft)
Iris	blue/white/yellow	10–20 cm (4–8 in)
Muscari Grape hyacinth	blue	15–20 cm (6–8 in)
Narcissus Daffodil	yellow/white/pink shades	15–60 cm (6 in–2 ft)
Tulipa Tulip	red/white/orange/ pink/yellow	15–60 cm (6 in—2 ft)

13. SUMMER FLOWERING BULBS

Name	Flower	Height	Spread
Anemone	red/blue/white	30–60 cm (1–2 ft)	30 cm (1 ft)
Crocosmia Montbretia	red/yellow/orange	30–90 cm (1–3 ft)	30 cm (1 ft)
Gladiolus	white/red/pink	30–90 cm (1–3 ft)	15–20 cm (6–8 in)
Lilium Lilies	white/pink/yellow/ orange	45 cm–1.2 m (1½–4 ft)	30 cm (1 ft)

14. HERBS AND FRAGRANT PLANTS

Name	Flower/foliage	Season	Height	Spread
Angelica	white	summer	1.5 m (5 ft)	60–90 cm (2–3 ft)
Anthriscus Chervil	green foliage	summer	30–45 cm (1–1½ ft)	30 cm (1 ft)
Artemesia Tarragon	grey/green fol.	summer	45–60 cm (1½–2 ft)	30 cm (1 ft)
Borago Borage	blue	summer	45–75 cm (1½–2½ ft)	30 cm (1 ft)
Cytisus Broom	yellow/cream	summer	60 cm–1.5 m (2–5 ft)	45–60 cm (1½–2 ft)
Foeniculum Fennel	green/purple fol.	summer	60–75 cm (2–2½ ft)	30–45 cm (1–1½ ft)
Heliotropium Heliotrope	purple	summer	30–90 cm (1–3 ft)	30 cm (1 ft)
Hyssopus Hyssop	blue/pink	summer	30–45 cm (1–1½ ft)	30 cm (1 ft)
Lavandula Lavender	blue/purple	summer	30–60 cm (1–2 ft)	30–60 cm (1–2 ft)
Melissa Balm	green/gold fol.	summer	30–90 cm (1–3 ft)	30–45 cm (1–1½ ft)
Mentha Mint	green/purple/vari. fol.	summer	30–90 cm (1–3 ft)	30 cm (1 ft)
Ocimum Basil	green fol.	summer	30 cm (1 ft)	15–20 cm (6–8 in)
Origanum Marjoram	green/gold fol.	summer	30–60 cm (1–2 ft)	30 cm (1 ft)
Pteriselinum Parsley	green fol.	summer	30–45 cm (1–1½ ft)	30 cm (1 ft)
Reseda Mignonette	greenish yellow	summer	30 cm (1 ft)	20–30 cm (8 in–1 ft)
Rosmarinus Rosemary	blue	summer	45–90 cm (1½–3 ft)	30–45 cm (1–1½ ft)
Ruta Rue	blue-green fol.	all year	30–60 cm (1–2 ft)	30–45 cm (1–1½ ft)
Salvia Sage	blue/white	summer	45–60 cm (1½–2 ft)	30–45 cm (1–1½ ft)
Santolina Cotton lavender	green/grey fol.	all year	30–60 cm (1–2 ft)	30–45 cm (1–1½ ft)
Thymus Thyme	white/pink/red	summer	5–30 cm (2 in–1 ft)	15–30 cm (6 in–1 ft)
Viburnum	white/pink	winter/ spring	1.5–3 m (5–10 ft)	1.5–2 m (5–10 ft)

15. WILD FLOWERS

Name	Flower	Season	Height	Spread
Agrostemma Corn cockle	pink	summer	30–60 cm (1–2 ft)	30 cm (1 ft)
Anagallis Pimpernel	scarlet	summer	15 cm (6 in)	15–20 cm (6–8 in)
Caltha Marsh marigold	yellow	spring	30–45 cm (1–1½ ft)	30–45 cm (1–1½ ft)
Campanula Bell flower	blue/white	summer	15–45 cm (6 in–1½ ft)	30–45 cm (1–1½ ft)
Clematis Old man's beard	white	spring	climbing	
Digitalis Foxglove	purple	summer	45–75 cm (1½–2½ ft)	15–20 cm (6–8 in)
Filipendula Meadowsweet	white	summer	45–75 cm (1½–2½ ft)	20–30 cm (8 in–1 ft)
Fritillaria Fritillary	white/ purple	spring	20–30 cm (8 in–1 ft)	15 cm (6 in)
Hypericum St. John's wort	yellow	summer	30–60 cm (1–2 ft)	30 cm (1 ft)
Lychnis Ragged Robin	pink	summer	30–45 cm (1–1½ ft)	30 cm (1 ft)
Myosotis Forget-me-not	blue	spring	15–30 cm (6 in–1 ft)	15–20 cm (6–8 in)
Primula Primrose, cowslip	yellow	spring	15–20 cm (6–8 in)	15–20 cm (6–8 in)
Pulsatilla Pasque flower	purple	spring	30 cm (1 ft)	30 cm (1 ft)
Silene Campion	red/white	summer	30–45 cm (1–1½ ft)	30 cm (1 ft)
Succisa Devils bit scabious	lilac-blue	summer	45 cm (1½ ft)	30 cm (1 ft)
Torilis Hedge parsley	white	summer	30–60 cm (1–2 ft)	30 cm (1 ft)

16. PLANTS FOR WILDLIFE

Name	Flower/fruit	Season	Height	Spread
Borago Borage	blue	summer	45–75 cm (1½–2½ ft)	30 cm (1 ft)
Buddleia Butterfly bush	white/purple/blue	summer	2–4 m (6½–13 ft)	1.5–2 m (5–6½ ft)
Cotoneaster	red/yellow/orange fr.	autumn	45 cm–2.5 m (1½–8¼ ft)	60 cm–1.5 m (2–5 ft)
Dipsacus Teasel	seed heads	autumn	1–1.5 m (3¼–5 ft)	60 cm (2 ft)
Helianthus Sunflower	yellow	l. summer	1–2 m (3¼–6½ ft)	90 cm (3 ft)
Hyssopus Hyssop	blue/pink	summer	30–45 cm (1–1½ ft)	30 cm (1 ft)
Nepeta Catmint	pale blue	summer	30–45 cm (1–1½ ft)	30–45 cm (1–1½ ft)
Pyracantha Firethorn	red/orange fr.	autumn	1.5–2.5 m (5–8¼ ft)	1–1.5 m (3¼–5 ft)
Sedum Ice plant	pink	autumn	30–45 cm (1–1½ ft)	30–45 cm (1–1½ ft)

INDEX